Cream of the Crop

Tour Guide Tales from
Disneyland's Golden Years

Andrea McGann Keech

*To Dennis Dozier ~
Much appreciation for
the counseling and
support! :) Fondly ~
Andrea Keech*

Theme Park Press
www.ThemeParkPress.com

Editor: Bob McLain
Layout: Artisanal Text

ISBN 978-1-941500-98-9
Printed in the United States of America

Theme Park Press | **www.ThemeParkPress.com**
Address queries to bob@themeparkpress.com

To Ron,
Who lived this story with me:
I miss you every day

And to our children,
Liz and Rob:
So proud of you both

Contents

Prologue:
Step Right This Way

We wore dark blue velvet riding caps, red Pendleton wool knee socks, Royal Stewart tartan-plaid culottes cut to look like pleated skirts, and red vests over long-sleeved white blouses trimmed in lace, even when the mercury soared above 100 degrees, and we carried actual leather riding crops from England.

How many times were we asked, "Where's your horse?"

Well, how many hidden Mickeys are there in Walt Disney World?

I started working as a Disney tour guide and VIP hostess during Christmas break of 1969 when I was just eighteen, the youngest tour guide on the Disneyland staff, and I worked throughout my college vacations until I graduated and became a teacher who told Disney tales to generations of students eager to hear the inside story. It was a dream I'd had—to work for Disney—for as long as I could remember. I still have the kind answer letter received when I wrote as a young student myself, asking, "How many more years do I have to wait until I can go to work at Disneyland?"

At Disneyland's 15th birthday party on July 17, 1970, we tour guides handed out carnations at the front gate to all the guests who visited that day. I saved my flower's paper backing, the happy 15th birthday card, attached behind the flower long before I even knew the meaning of the word *ephemera*. In fact, I saved just about everything including the (gasp) official tour guide training manual, a sacred artifact I simply couldn't bring myself to relinquish. I retained my eleven-page tour guide spiel in both English and Spanish, tour guide banquet program, the banquet's skit script complete with gentle "roasts" of Disney higher-ups and cast members alike, unused tickets from the 1950s and 1960s, maps with rides now just memories (I was one of those unlucky enough to get a "flying" saucer that remained stuck to the ground throughout the entire length of the ride), copies of *Backstage* magazines, and *Disneyland Line* newsletters. If it was delivered into my hands, I held onto it! I loved everything Disney, and working at the park really was my dream come true.

The tour guides were made to feel very special from our induction into the University of Disneyland (now called Disney University) until we proudly led that first tour on our own. During the summer of 1970, we trained the Florida kids, those grand Floridians who would become the first employees at Walt Disney World the following year when it opened. They job-shadowed us for weeks learning the ropes.

I was there on August 6 when a mass invasion of Hippies and Yippies snaked down Main Street and staged a take-over of Tom Sawyer island, smoking pot in the island's cave and Fort Wilderness, and running up the flag of North Vietnam on the island's flagpole. They chanted slogans about Ho Chi Minh while some of the guests sang "God Bless America" back at them. Before things got out of hand, the Orange County police in full riot gear appeared to quell the rebellion. It was the only time to that point when the park had to be closed during regular business hours for an unplanned event. We tour guides were told to lie flat on the floor of the little tour guide office so that we couldn't be seen through the windows by any stray, marauding hippies. It was incredibly exciting and very scary at the same time. We were hustled out the back entrance to the parking lot, but the next day it was back to business as usual.

The dress codes in those years were quaintly hilarious by today's standards. I once had our lead girl, who would later head the whole department of Walt Disney World tour guides, stick a ruler into my Gibson Girl hairdo to be sure it was no higher than two inches! The guys' sideburns could be no longer than mid-ear. One of my VIP tours with a well-known folk singer and her agent had to be held up while her too-scruffy-for-Disneyland date, also a singer but a lot less well-known, was forced to either leave or purchase a park-friendly T-shirt *sans* holes. He bought the shirt. Men were not admitted wearing sleeveless muscle shirts, either, although we often saw women sporting a full head of pink, plastic curlers. I always wondered where they were going *after* they went to Disneyland.

The guides were an elite group. One of our fellow tour guides had been crowned Miss Universe the year before joining our ranks, and many of the girls were veterans of the local beauty pageant circuits. Several went on to become Disney Ambassadors traveling the world representing the public face of the company. One perfectly delightful girl voted Tour Guide of the Year is still routinely featured in major business magazines for her acumen and expertise in the corporate world.

Out of every thousand applicants who wanted to work in the park, just one was granted the right to wield the coveted riding crop that marked her status as a tour guide. It took four interviews, the final one with the formidable Cicely Rigdon, the supervisor of Guest Relations, before you were inducted into that extremely select club, one even more exclusive than the park's private Club 33 where we dined on lobster with our VIP guests.

It was a golden age when Disneyland and we were young, a time when working alongside six thousand other employees, half of whom were "seasonal" employees working through their college vacations like me, really was the best of times. Join me for a fond look at the way we did things at the park back when Walt Disney World was just a brilliant idea and 27,000 acres of Florida swampland. Come on folks, step right this way....

When You Wish Upon a Star

If you had grown up as I did in the 1950s in the shadow of Disneyland, you would have probably dreamed of working there one day, too. The park first opened its doors to the invited guests on July 17, 1955 (the day before it opened to the general public), when I was four years old. Although my family didn't receive an invitation and wasn't among the well-connected hordes that descended upon the "Happiest Place on Earth" on that legendary first day, we could be counted among the first people to visit that summer.

You have only to watch videos of the first chaotic day to understand why my parents wisely chose to wait a couple of weeks before taking the plunge. Plumbing strikes and extremely limited rest room facilities, just-laid pavement literally melting underfoot in the baking California sun, and kinks and glitches enough to turn Walt's hair gray(er) were part and parcel of Disneyland's opening day jitters. We visited the park later in that summer of 1955 and every summer thereafter. We visited many falls, winters, and springs, as well, until at last I was able to fulfill my very own wish-upon-a-star and enter Disneyland by the back door as a newly minted cast member.

An early, hopeful letter I sent to the park asking how old I needed to be to work at Disneyland was very kindly answered, just the first small gesture of many that would forever impress upon me the thoughtful Disney way of doing things:

July 15, 1966

Dear Andrea,

This is in reply to your recent inquiry regarding employment at Disneyland.

We are sorry to inform you that our minimum hiring age is 18 yrs. of age.

We sincerely appreciate the interest that prompted you to contact Disneyland.

Cordially,

Chas. T. Whelan

Personal Supervisor

I would have to bide my time and wait, which I did—impatiently. In the meantime, my cousin was hired for summer work as a street sweeper. He came home with stories of backstage hilarity and insider insights that only whetted my appetite for joining the cast one day, and the sooner the better. University of Disneyland. Canoe races around Tom Sawyer Island before early morning shifts. Baseball leagues with competitions among cast members. Beach parties. House parties. It sounded almost too good to be true.

He sometimes worked until 2:00 a.m. in the summer or until the park closed. Once, he swept up a twenty dollar bill, a highlight of the week when he was paid less than two dollars an hour. Late one evening, he reported running into Walt Disney who was walking alone through the park just after closing time.

"Hi, Walt."

"Hello, Matt."

Walt Disney didn't actually know my cousin by name. No one, no matter how involved in the workings of an organization, could have known each of the six thousand employees by name, but cast members and executives alike all wear name badges with first names printed in easily visible large block letters. If you slipped and called someone "Mister," you would be coolly and firmly told that the name is Dick or Ron or Walt, not Mr. Nunis, Mr. Dominguez, and most assuredly not Mr. Disney.

That was the extent of their interchange, but what a moment! It took place in the summer of 1966, about half a year before Walt's death. My cousin explained that in the Disney organization, only first names were ever used, even with the big boss himself. The job sounded every bit as exciting as I had always imagined it would be, and I speculated on which position I'd most like to have every single time we visited.

The attractions operators, for the most part, had very cool costumes, and their jobs seemed interesting. My cousin's girlfriend was one of the singing waitresses during the summer of 1966 at the Golden Horseshoe Revue in Frontierland, but I couldn't carry a tune. Therefore, that option was most definitely out, even though the costumes the waitresses wore were dance hall girl glamorous. It never even crossed my mind that I might possibly be cast as a (gulp) food service worker or land a position in (shudder) retail sales. Girls weren't sweepers at that time, so there was no chance getting stuck with Matt's menial job, although he never saw it that way. He loved

1213 HARBOR BLVD., ANAHEIM, CALIF. 92803 · TELEPHONES: KEystone 3-4456 AND MAdison 6-8805

July 15, 1966

Andrea McGann
10619 Sunnybrook Lane
Whittier, Calif.

Dear Andrea:

This is in reply to your recent inquiry regarding employment at Disneyland.

We are sorry to have to inform you that our minimum hiring age is 18 years of age.

We sincerely appreciate the interest that prompted you to contact Disneyland.

Cordially,
DISNEYLAND

Chas. T. Whelan

C. T. WHELAN
Personnel Supervisor

CTW:ls

every minute of it, but he still gamely memorized the Jungle Boat skippers' spiel in hopes of switching to Operations one day.

That day never came, although he did get a chance or two to cover when they were short-handed over at Jungle. The handsome, khaki safari suits and rakishly angled, wide-brimmed hats trimmed with faux zebra or leopard skin must have been a nice switch from the boxy, nondescript sweeper whites he normally wore. Those Jungle Boat skippers were as handsome as their costumes, and yes, they most certainly did know it. It was one of the most highly coveted positions for guys at that time because it required personally interacting with guests, memorizing an extensive spiel, delivering it with humor, and looking absolutely dashing all the while. They even had their own end-of-summer bash, the Banana Ball, just as the tour guides always had our own banquet. I doubt, however, if Rock Cornish game hens and wild rice stuffing were served at the Banana Ball. Long before I was ever hired, it was clearly apparent that there was a definite hierarchy among park cast members, and I began mentally narrowing my options.

You will often hear it said that you don't cast yourself at Disneyland, you are cast, but that wasn't my experience. From the time I wrote my letter until I was finally hired three years later, I formulated a strategy for being placed in a position I was fairly confident that I would enjoy. Pay matched responsibility at Disneyland, just as it does in most corporations. The Jungle Boat skippers were paid more than the sweepers. The monorail operators out-earned the food servers working at Carousel Corner. At the very peak of the social pyramid of some three thousand of the park's seasonal employees hired during college vacations were the tour guides and VIP hostesses. By the time I was hired, the guides and VIP hostesses had become one in the same. Even though most girls did mainly one or the other, you had to be ready to do either at a moment's notice.

Guides weren't limited to hanging out in any one land. They were able to roam freely about the park. It might be earth-shattering, or at the very least illusion-destroying, for guests to see a Western cowpoke strolling through Tomorrowland or a space-age PeopleMover operator hanging out in Fantasyland, but tour guides could go anywhere and everywhere; best of all, guides were actually paid to take scores of happy guests on the rides! After working during my last break at a national fast food chain for $1.05 an hour, the $2.20 starting salary for tour guides sounded positively princely. I was even paid an extra nickel an hour for being able to lead tours in Spanish, but more about that challenge later. Long before I sought a job at Disneyland, it was easy to see that the tour guide costumes were the cutest ones for girls in the park by miles.

Today, you sometimes hear guides referred to as "plaids," a moniker perhaps meant to take them down a peg in the same way successful business executives might be referred to as "suits." What we wore was a lot more than simply plaid, though. It was the Royal Stewart tartan handed down from the ancient Scottish kings, the same tartan still worn by Queen Elizabeth II, and which all her subjects are entitled to wear, a fabric woven over centuries by some of history's bravest warriors into the great tapestry of Britain. Plaids, indeed. *Harumph.*

Plaids was not a term in use when I finally reached that magical age of eighteen and applied for seasonal employment in November of 1969, my freshman year of college. I hoped to beat the crush of applicants in May, to work over the winter holidays, and be trained and ready to go by the time summer rolled around. Timing, as it so often is, was critical, and my strategy paid off. By then, I had narrowed my hopes down to two positions: tour guide or waitress in the Blue Bayou Restaurant in New Orleans Square. The latter made the final cut not because of the costume, a long, pale blue dress, but because of the potential for earning extremely good tips. Apart from the private Club 33, the Bayou was the most expensive dining establishment in the park.

November 25, 1969

Miss Andrea McGann
Box 145 - Occidental College
1600 Campus Road
Los Angeles, California   90041

Dear Andrea:

Thank you for your letter of November 20, 1969. We sincerely
appreciate your interest.

The Application you requested in your letter is enclosed
along with one of our Fact Sheets. Please read the Fact
Sheet thoroughly. After completing the Application form,
please return it to me. You will hear from us again,
shortly.

Thank you again, Andrea, for your interest in Disneyland.

Very truly yours,

DISNEYLAND

B. W. Hansen
Personnel Manager

BWH:dr

Enclosures

After years of biding my time, I was ready to apply. It's difficult to overestimate how competitive it was getting a seasonal job, *any* seasonal job, back in 1969. The Baby Boomer demographic was the elephant in the room, a time when ten people might apply for one opening at McDonald's. It was hard getting *any* employment let alone a really cool job like working at Disneyland. Millions of people lived in southern California, and at any moment thousands of them were the right age for Disneyland seasonal employment.

The first thing I did was call Disneyland Information, phones I would soon be answering myself, to request information. The company sent me an application and an informative booklet, *Casting for a Role in Our Disneyland Show*. In it, Mickey Mouse cheerfully advised potential applicants:

> Since we have a summer cast of nearly 6,000 people, we'd like to save you as much time as possible and make the casting procedure as easy as we can for you. We are outlining key points in our casting procedure to give you a better understanding of our casting process.

If you don't read and then carefully follow directions, in other words, more fool you.

CASTING for a ROLE IN OUR Disneyland SHOW

The pretty little pink-and-white illustrated folder went on to inform potential applicants, "...you are not really being 'hired' for a job, rather, we are 'casting' you for a role in the show." This, for many people, was their first introduction to park-speak. My cousin had already clued me in to some of the Disney vernacular. Disneyland is a "world renowned theme spectacular," it is most definitely *not* an amusement park. We are entertainers, not employees. It's a show, not a job. You are playing a part, wearing a costume, learning your lines. That all sounded pretty darned sweet—especially after slinging greasy chicken legs and gravy during my previous school break.

There was no sugar coating of Disney's expectations, however. We would work while our family and friends played. This fact would hit home especially hard when I had to work on Christmas Day the very next month! The brochure specified that "extroverts who can work with people on a highly personalized basis" were desired. I had always been extremely studious and had even been voted the "most studious senior girl" in my high school class of five hundred. I was also definitely on the shy side, so this would be an area for me to improve upon. Like an actress preparing for a new role, I'd simply have to convincingly pretend to be an extrovert.

This was the first, but far from the last, time I had heard about the "Disneyland Look." If I wanted to get hired, *ahem*, I mean *cast*, I needed to be neat, enthusiastic, friendly, polite, poised, have a pleasant personality, have reliable transportation, and be available. Whew! That was a fairly tall order, and given my naturally reserved, quiet demeanor, there would be a lot to work on before my first interview.

No one vertically or horizontally challenged need apply. "Due to wardrobe limitations," and more importantly but never actually stated—physical attractiveness—hostesses must be between 5'2" and 5'10" and wear size 6–14. (Please note that size 6 in 1969 was considerably smaller than it is today!) Hosts must wear jackets between 36-44, pants (called "trousers") with a waist of 28–40 and a length of 28–35. Period. Every guy in the realistic cartoon drawings illustrating the booklet was a square-jawed hunk, every girl a vision of loveliness. They didn't have to say so explicitly. It was pretty clear exactly the type of cast members they were looking for. Although applicants were advised that "there is no maximum age limit," everyone in the illustrations looked to be about twenty-one.

There would be a personal interview where "we try to be as fair as we can," the booklet reassured applicants. Potential cast members would be rated on various "factors" and selection made from "those who most closely" fit the bill. They would contact all applicants, regardless of whether they were selected, a good way to do business and one every organization should emulate.

During that initial, critical evaluation, useful tips were given on what to do and how to do it, advice that still applies for today's job market every bit as well as it did in 1969:

- Be well prepared for the interview.

- Be on time. Allow enough time for emergencies to be sure that you are on time for your scheduled interview.

- Be sure that you have filled out your application completely. Have your driver's license and your Social Security card on hand. (They weren't kidding about the need to prove you'd passed your 18th birthday milestone!) Know the days and times when you will be available to work.

- Be enthusiastic.

- Always put your best foot forward and show yourself in the best light possible when you come in for an interview—be natural, be yourself.

It ended with a big, encouraging: "THANKS AGAIN FOR YOUR INTEREST!"

tips for JOB INTERVIEWING AT Disneyland

CASTING TIPS

If this is your first time out as a job hunter in the business world, here are a few tips that may make the process much easier...

Prepare for the interview   Punctuality is essential - allow adequate time for emergencies and make sure that you are on time for your scheduled interview   Make sure that your application is complete   Bring your driver's license and social security card... • Know when you're going to be available   Be enthusiastic   Present yourself in the best light when you come in for an interview - be natural, be yourself.

THANKS AGAIN FOR YOUR INTEREST!

DISNEYLAND EMPLOYMENT DEPARTMENT   An Equal Opportunity Employer

D-723 R-1

You'd better believe I prepared for my interview. I can still remember how exciting it was pulling up to the gate at the employee's entrance and being directed to the "visitor" section. As many times as I'd been to the park, I had never actually noticed that gate before, just as I hadn't noticed the many discreetly positioned doors that exist throughout Disneyland leading to backstage. I wore a new conservative dress, nude stockings, low heels, just a little make-up, no jewelry, and had my hair in curls. My cousin told me that all female cast members were required to have curls. Straight hair was never permitted.

I parked for the first time in the big employee parking lot, now just a memory after the construction of Space Mountain in 1977, and headed over to the glass doors in the long, low, cream-colored building that held the reception area. As I walked, I was surrounded by the crush of people coming and going to and from their shifts in the park. It was a busy, happy group, for the most part, and I curiously looked at them all, hoping very soon I'd be counted among their ranks. I had been advised to bring a resume, which was carefully read by Jack, the handsome young man who interviewed me. He had the Disneyland Look coming out his ears.

When he asked me what kinds of things I might be interested in doing if I were hired, I said, "Either a tour guide or a waitress at the Blue Bayou." He seemed a bit surprised by my ready answer.

"Those are the two things I know I'd enjoy and be good at. I've been thinking about this job for years." Know exactly what you want and ask for it, I figured. I went on to tell him how long I had waited for this very moment and about my letter to Personnel asking how soon I could apply, a small detail but one that seemed to please him quite a bit. I did my best to pretend I was an extrovert, smiling, chatting away, acting like I was having the time of my life.

As I got up to leave at the end of our conversation, he said, "Wait. You're going to go to another interview."

"Now?" This was unexpected, but at least it seemed a promising development.

"Yes, right now. I'll walk you over to Jay, who'll be interviewing you next."

Different guy, similar interview. By now, I was feeling more relaxed, settling back, and even beginning to enjoy the process a little. The people I had met so far were encouraging and very, very nice. I started to get excited about the direction in which things were heading.

When I stood up from my chair opposite Jay's desk to leave after the second interview, he said, "Wait, I want you to meet John. He'll have a few more questions for you."

Three interviews in one afternoon is a lot, even for an extrovert, which I definitely wasn't; this was getting to be an awful lot of smiling and talking about myself and the things I hoped to do if I were hired, I mean *cast*.

I thought my interview this afternoon might take about half an hour to forty-five minutes at most.

It had been a couple of hours already, and now John was telling me, "I think it's time for you to meet Cicely." After Jack, Jay, and John, I assumed this "Cicely" fellow must be of Italian descent.

John ushered me into a comfortably furnished office, larger by far than the three previous ones. Behind the desk sat an impeccably groomed woman of middle years. Every hair, and I mean *every* hair, was firmly in place. She was dressed like a First Lady, and in a way, I suppose she was—the First Lady of Disneyland Guest Relations.

John handed her my now well-thumbed resume, and she smiled at me briefly, saying, "Hello, Andrea, my name is Cicely," in the most cultivated, British accent you can imagine. "Please, take a seat."

Oh. That kind of Cicely.

The three J's had been mere warm-up acts. This was the real deal, the interview that would determine whether my wish really would come true.

Cicely took a minute to glance over my resume, set it down on the desk, and looked at me with piercing, serious blue eyes. "Well, we're quite the person, aren't we?"

After that particularly dismal opening, our conversation had nowhere to go but up.

About a week later, I got the call informing me that my orientation and tour guide training would begin at the start of winter break. I was in!

Cicely Rigdon astride a cannon

A Degree from the University of Disneyland

"Andrea, can I ask a question? Is that your real hair?" the energetic young instructor asked me the first night after class. He didn't do this in front of the entire group. He was considerate enough to wait until things had wrapped up for the evening. The newest class of Disney coeds was gathering up materials, getting out of their seats, and starting to bustle through the door.

"You know, it looks great," said the woman instructor standing beside him nodding and smiling brightly, "really great! We've been debating between ourselves all night about whether or not it was real. We just couldn't tell for sure."

Happy to provide you both with so many busy hours of speculation. Yikes.

"Well, the top part is mine and the bottom part is a fall," I told them, wondering uneasily if I were about to be fired before ever working a single day at the park. "All of these are mine," I said, running my fingers through the tightly curled ringlets around my face, tugging them like a kid pulling on Santa's beard, to prove it.

"Okay," the personable male instructor nodded, confirming his suspicions.

"You know that you aren't allowed to wear any kind of hairpieces while you're working at Disneyland, right?" the female instructor asked me. These restrictions, of course, didn't apply to Alice, Snow White, Cinderella, Tinker Bell, or the girls at the Golden Horseshoe Revue.

"Yes, I do now. I heard that tonight. Sorry!"

Did it really matter during training class? I certainly wasn't trying to pull a fast one or anything like that. Those of us who had just been hired to work during the busy winter holiday season were meeting in the Administration Building for three nights of orientation. We weren't anywhere near paying guests, we weren't even technically inside the park itself, but this incident just goes to show how seriously, how *very* seriously, Disney took its hair policies.

"No, don't worry. It doesn't matter for now. We just want to make sure you know that you can't wear it when you're working in the park," he told me intently.

"Okay, I understand. Thanks." I picked up my notebook and materials and turned to leave.

"But it looks *really* great!" the woman called as I left.

It did.

It is impossible to overestimate the importance of hair, the starring role hair played, and people's preoccupation with all things hair-related in 1969 when I enrolled at the U. of D., not only here but in the outside world as well. For the entire decade of the 1960s and well beyond, ladies' hairpieces were not just popular, they were a phenomenon. I had three of them.

There was the wiglet, a small circle of about eight or ten fat, rolled-under curls. It wasn't a full wig. Those can be hot and itchy. Winglets were worn on the crown of the head like a little pillbox hat you might see on Jackie Kennedy, except that in this case the hat would be made of curls. Practically everyone had them. Even girls with very short hair wore them perched on top of their heads; it appeared as though they had cut only the front and back fringe of their hair short while letting the central part grow extremely long, making it resemble the exact opposite of a monk's tonsure.

Then came the fall, a little half-wig of straight or curled hair you attached to the top of your head by the small comb sewn into it. For added verisimilitude, you brought up the front part of your hair around it and fastened it at the top with a clip or bow or a tied ribbon.

This was what had attracted the scrutiny of my U. of D. instructors on the first night of class. Mine was virtually undetectable from the real thing. The only tip-off was that it looked a little too good to be real. Real hair is never that impossibly thick or luxurious. Long strands of my own hair had been curled and fell over the top of it. Lots of small curls, the ringlets I pulled to demonstrate their authenticity, framed my face.

My aunt was a hairdresser and knew her stuff. All of my hairpieces had been expertly dyed to perfectly match my own hair, right down to the three or four white hairs I'd been born with. She was that good. In addition to the shoulder-length fall, I also had one that went down my back past the shoulder blades. They were called falls because they resembled a waterfall of hair. A not-as-popular kind of hairpiece was the cascade. That one, I didn't have. It was an alliance between the wiglet and the fall, tight curls on top with increasingly looser ones descending downward like—well, a cascade. Other than Elizabeth Taylor, not many people could successfully pull off wearing a cascade.

Every time we watched a movie or television program together, my aunt would say, "See that? She's wearing a wig." A few minutes would pass. "That redhead's got on a wiglet." Shortly thereafter, you might hear, "Oh, and that blonde has a fall. Look at that shine on it. It isn't even human hair. The color isn't a very good match, either." It was like watching a program but only fixating on the actresses' hair instead of the plot. Eventually, I got where I could spot a wig or hairpiece a mile away. I still can.

Watching films made in the 1960s is the only way for you to fully appreciate what I'm describing. It doesn't matter if it's a Western, a World War II action movie, or a flapper flick set in the Roaring 20s. No matter what, women of the 60s stubbornly, tenaciously clung to 60s hairstyles, regardless of the time period they might have been portraying on the screen. Anything else seemed unthinkable, apparently, because all you'll see are wiglets, falls, and maybe a cascade if Liz Taylor is starring.

Hairpieces were positively ubiquitous in Disney films. The best example of why a full wig is so rarely the right choice may be found in Disney's 1961 Hayley Mills showcase, *The Parent Trap*. As twin Susan, she wears a bad fall, and as twin Sharon she wears an uncomfortable looking Dutch Boy wig. Picture a hairy little shower cap. How could her *own* hair have possibly been any worse? You can see just a bit of it above the fall before Susan gets sheared. Someone on the movie set could have, *should* have, pointed out the obvious.

A friend of mine in high school had a long, false pony tail. It was called a *postiche*, the French word for wig, and it was the least common of the 60s hairpieces. I can easily see her jogging in PE class in front of me as we cycled through the strenuous set of daily RCAF calisthenics. That's right, kids. We did the same exercises as the Royal Canadian Air Force, we didn't play ping pong. Jog-jog-jog. It swung hypnotically from side to side. The swaying pony tail ultimately slipped the surly bonds of earth, leapt high into the air, fell back to the pavement, and settled docilely at her feet like a pocket pet. She bent down without missing a beat, grabbed it, and stuck it in the pocket of her gym shorts. Jog-jog-jog. It peeked out, a shy blonde ferret, until class ended and it could be again firmly pinned to her head.

Today, hair extensions are a popular trend, the heirs apparent to the hairpieces of the 60s and 70s. Nearly all of the female news anchors you'll ever see wear them, and so do most actresses and singers. They make your hair look twice as good as it otherwise would. Some take it a step too far. Brittany Spears and the notorious meltdown involving scissors comes to mind. One of our unfortunate local anchor women looks as though, without her awareness or consent, a raccoon has curled up and gone to sleep on top of her head. I feel pretty confident that hair extensions are not an acceptable part of the current Disneyland Look.

At the University of Disneyland, Class of '69, we talked about hair more than just about any other single topic. Men's hair length, ladies' hair length, no bizarre dye jobs for either sex, the permitted ladies' hair height, the fact that "body" or curls were required for ladies at all times, no backcombing (more popularly known as "ratting")—there was just no end to the many ways you could manage to violate the strict hair codes. You weren't allowed to frost or streak or bleach or tint your hair, either. There were literally pages written, printed, and distributed to us on the subject.

Hair wasn't just a preoccupation at dear old U. of D., either. On one of our fancier dates, Ron took me to see the play *Hair* in Los Angeles at the Aquarius Theatre. It was naughtily notorious because of a nano-second nude scene at the end. The title song in the show was a paean to the glories of long hair:

> Give me down to there,
> Hair!
> Shoulder length and longer,
> Hair, Baby,
> Hair, Mama,
> Everywhere, Daddy, Daddy,
> Hair!

Another line in this song just repeated the word "hair" four times in a row. Believe it or not, people honestly paid money to see this. I wore a floor-length, forest-green dress with silver sandals. Before the curtain went up, roving characters from the play initiated some playful audience interactions. Dangling from above us in the theatre's rafters, a sartorially savvy hippie with miles of long, lustrous curls threw a real daisy into my lap and asked, "Is that dress velvet?" When I nodded in the affirmative, he kindly observed, "It's beautiful." Hippies could be sweet.

Hair determined your political affiliation, whether you were counter-culture or establishment, and even what kind of music you were into. The Beatles may have started the long hair obsession, but it grew to encompass every aspect of American society in the Swingin' Sixties.

Even the end-of-summer tour guide banquet in 1971 had its closing song devoted to hair, or rather the lack of same, with original lyrics set to the same tune as the little ditty above. Instead of extolling the virtues of hair, though, its refrain was "Nair" in honor of a personal hygiene product that removed unwanted hair:

> Gimme, gimme Nair
> Spray can or foam,
> Cream or lotion,
> I don't really care,
> Nair, Nair, Nair, Nair

While hair was the star, there were plenty of supporting players in the Disneyland Look. Make-up, jewelry, fingernails, perfume—they were all meticulously regulated. The Wardrobe Department devoted two pages to women's shoes alone. At the U. of D., we tour guides were advised in Bulletin 15 to purchase black shoes with 1" to 2" heels. Tiki room hostesses had to buy brown sandals with open toes and "flat to 2-inch heels." Did you work at Haunted Mansion or Pirates? Black flats for you, Missy. Every role in the Disneyland show called for its own kind of shoes. There was a store near the park that sold the best ones, and that's where we all went. You needed comfortable shoes if you were going to criss-cross seventy-some acres all day, every day.

During night school at the university, we received yet another bulletin from Wardrobe with stern admonitions about how to check out and turn in our costumes. Most of this was written in all caps, the modern equivalent of screaming online. Wardrobe wanted you to be absolutely, positively sure you knew the severe penalties awaiting you, should you fail to turn in EVERY PART of your costume. It was like those tags attached to pillows that threaten "do not remove under penalty of law." We all remove them, but we feel slightly guilty when doing so.

I recently asked a friend who had worked at Florida's Magic Kingdom, "Did you ever know anyone who turned in their name tag when they left?"

After she finished laughing and was finally able to catch her breath, she said, "No."

In the Disneyland Look packet, it explicitly says that if you lose your name tag, you will be charged the cost of replacement. If only Disneyland could collect on all those unpaid debts over the last sixty years, it could just about double its bottom line. The bulletin also advised us: PLEASE WEAR IT. Everyone wanted to wear their name tag. That wasn't the problem. It's just that people didn't want to turn loose of it when they left.

As I write, there are thousands of old name tags sitting safely tucked away in drawers all over the country, tangible reminders of the years we spent as tour guides, attractions operators, parking lot attendants, sweepers, RETLAW guys, and doing every other kind of assignment you can imagine and a few you probably can't. There must have been a couple of dutiful, unsentimental cast members who did turn in their name tags, though, because before they could print a tag up with my name, I had to wear one that erroneously claimed my name was Ann. There had either been no previous Andrea working at Disneyland, or no previous Andrea who had turned in her name tag when she left. (In case you're curious, I didn't, either.)

If anyone managed to graduate from the University of Disneyland without knowing all about the Disneyland Look, they must have been asleep at the wheel. The gist of it was this: always look neat and natural. No extremes of any kind would be tolerated. It's what used to be called "clean cut," but that term is also subjective. Like the Disneyland Look, though, you knew it when you saw it—or didn't.

We learned the specialized vocabulary we'd be expected to use on the job. These were the principle terms we had to master:

- guests
- hosts and hostesses
- show
- on stage
- backstage
- audience
- Disneylander
- costumes
- security officers (as opposed to guards)
- queues (as opposed to lines)
- attractions and adventures (as opposed to rides)
- the mandated use of first names

Everyone learned the terms and, for the most part, tried conscientiously to use them. The only term I've never heard used at *any* time by *anyone* is Disneylander. It is defined as a "unique cast member" who is "living that special life which we call Disneyland." If you called someone a Disneylander, I'd have thought you'd very likely end up dumped head-first into a passing sweeper's trash can.

In addition to mastering vocabulary, we were also warned about the Disney taboos, and most of these aren't just taboos at Disneyland, either. No fighting, falsification of records, gambling (occasional baseball pools excepted), drinking, stealing, or the catch-all "moral turpitude." Lesser sins included chewing gum (never sold in the park for obvious reasons), sleeping, smoking, arguing with or insulting a guest, and eating or taking breaks while on stage.

At the University of Disneyland, members of my class were given a beautiful, full-color training manual called *The Walt Disney Traditions at Disneyland*. It had been written in 1967. The traditions might seem like common sense, but it's amazing how effective they were in drawing the entire cast together. Teamwork was the goal, and that's what we learned in our classes. We were asked to treat every guest as a VIP, accept people as we found them, make guests feel they belong, be polite, give people individual attention whenever possible, and have a friendly smile. No one could possibly know answers to every question at a place as big as Disneyland, but if you didn't know, you were supposed to find out. In addition to all of this, we were asked to treat each other with the same consideration we gave our guests.

Roy Disney "personally" welcomed each and every one of us to the organization on page two. He had sat through the same training classes, he wrote, just as we were doing right now. In 1955, those classes had been personally taught by the famous employee training expert Van France himself. In his welcome, Roy immediately sets the tone maintained throughout all of our training. Van might have been the primary author of the publication, but Roy let us all know in no uncertain terms that our job, the reason why we were hired, was to help make other people happy. In the few short paragraphs, the word "dream" or "dreams" is repeated eight times. Roy left no doubt that we were in the business of making dreams come true. Yes, we might occasionally have a bad day, but we were asked to make sure every guest had a *good* one.

In my teaching years, I would occasionally encounter a student teacher who would say something along the lines of this: "I love modern poetry, so *that's* what I want to teach." I had to let the person know as carefully and tactfully as I could that teaching isn't ever about you, it's about your students. You don't teach what you want, you teach what they need. At Disneyland, you meet the needs of your guests, not your own. That was a lesson I learned at U. of D., and one I never forgot. It's not about *you*.

By 1971, my second summer as a tour guide, the Traditions publication was no longer in color, and it had been retitled *Your Role in the Disneyland Show*. Dick Nunis, Vice President of Disneyland Operations, wrote the "Welcome to the Cast" introduction. I did a quick tally counting seventy-three ellipsis periods in the handbook, and it's not very long. It is entirely probable that I missed a few. I enjoy using that mark of punctuation, too, but no one, and I mean *no one*, used ellipsis periods like Van. They were the merry confetti sprinkled throughout his writing. It is possible to tell exactly which sections of the booklet he had personally written by noting the liberal use of ellipsis periods.

In a later chapter of this book that describes the Yippie invasion of Disneyland, you'll be reminded of Timothy Leary's famous quote urging students to "tune in, turn on, drop out." This is Professor Van's Disneyfied version: "tune in...turn on...get with it..." By "turn on," I can say beyond a shadow of a doubt that Van France was *not* using the phrase in the same way Professor Leary did.

Van's style is endearing. He cared sincerely and passionately about training good, effective cast members. How else could could we make all of those dreams come true? Another page is headed "Practices...Procedures...

Policies...That sort of thing..." You can't accomplish the things he did without having complete confidence in your message. Van was a true original, one of those rare individuals who left his indelible stamp on the Disney way of doing things. I only wish I had known him personally, but he was no longer doing day-to-day (or night-to-night) teaching at the University of Disneyland by the time I enrolled.

The book of Traditions included four pages of quotations from Walt Disney himself about practically every topic you can imagine. About his employees, Walt says, "We train them to be aware that they're mainly here to help the guests." It was relentlessly drilled into us from the very first night of class.

That concept apparently takes a bit of adjusting to for some current cast members. Last winter, my daughter and her family and I traveled to Walt Disney World, one of our all-time favorite vacation destinations. Buzz Lightyear is a very popular attraction there. It's an interactive video game with neon-bright colors, flashing lights, and lots of sensory overload. As my granddaughter and I got off our small car, my first time on the attraction, I looked around for the EXIT. A host stood there staring straight ahead, his expression deadpan.

"Which way should we go?" I asked him.

He pointed to the stairs where there was, indeed, a little EXIT sign posted. He didn't say "duh" but might as well have done so. The eye-rolling, heavy sigh, and emphatic flip of his head toward the sign were not exactly guest friendly. Someone in charge had thought it would be helpful to have an actual person stand there to guide people unfamiliar with the attraction away from the disembarking area. If all they needed were a sign, he would not have been posted there. He was being paid to help but acted as if we were imposing on him. He definitely needed a refresher course at the university.

A similar incident happened at the monorail station outside the Polynesian Village Resort following a delightful 'Ohana character breakfast, something I highly recommend if you visit Walt Disney World. We usually boarded the monorail in the Contemporary Resort near our suite of rooms in the Bay Lake Tower. Because that's the monorail's first stop, we were used to encountering mostly empty cars. These cars were practically full; we stood ready to board with two young children and a very large number of other guests.

"Is there usually more room in the back cars?" I called over to the smartly-uniformed attendant standing near us on the platform, an attendant who had seen those same cars pass by about every ten or fifteen minutes of his shift. Since this was his assignment, it would be reasonable to assume he might have some degree of familiarity with which cars might be more likely to contain room and which wouldn't at this time of day.

"Why don't you go check and see?" he replied. The smirk didn't help. Neither did the dripping sarcasm.

I looked at him steadily. "Thanks."

When you realize that the *only* reason you are getting a paycheck is to help the guests, you simply don't treat them that way. Again, a refresher course was needed.

The final example I'll share of a Walt Disney World employee missing the point of why he had been hired was when we entered the enormous theatre to see the popular new *Frozen* live-action show. My granddaughter adores all things *Frozen* and went as Elsa for Halloween. We had splurged on a ridiculously gorgeous, elaborate costume for her. Even Elsa herself, during a meet-and-greet photo session later, commented on how incredible the outfit was when they met. She could have passed for Elsa's little sister. Oh, wait, that's Anna. Let's just say our sweet little seven year old looked every inch the sparkly snow princess. There were still many good seats open down front. We had arrived early enough in order to get as close as we could to the stage. As we sat down, a cast member came over.

"You can't sit there!" he barked at us loudly. "That section's reserved!"

No sign was apparent. On the way out following the performance, I looked for and saw the little sign we had missed. It was posted at the back of the section. We had come in at the front.

"Where should we sit?"

"Over there." He waved vaguely in the direction of the side of the big auditorium.

Shortly thereafter, two teenaged girls walked up to the same host and asked him if they could sit down in front. By this time we had found decent seats, close enough to overhear the following exchange.

"They're reserved," he said, flashing them a big smile.

"How about if we give you a hug?" one asked, returning the smile.

"Okay," he grinned.

Both girls gave him full-body, protracted hugs and then, giggling, took seats in the area we had just vacated. A good deal of the audience was made up of young girls. What message was that host sending?

One of the sacrosanct Disney traditions is that *everyone* is a VIP. Either Disney is relaxing its requirements for grads of the U. of D. these days, supervisory standards have slipped, or maybe it's just that people have a lot more employment options than we did.

Being on the guest side of things instead of the cast side makes it easy to see that while the intentions of the cast training program are undoubtedly good, there are times like these when a refresher course is most definitely called for. We encountered, of course, good employees who were helpful and professional over the duration of our most recent visit, but the three

I've just described are unfortunately the ones who made the strongest impression. In the first two cases, the hosts had acted annoyed and snarky when asked a simple question, and in the last case, the host's behavior was inappropriate. Those are the kinds of cast *faux pas* that would have made steam come out of Walt's ears, had he witnessed them. A letter I sent to three top Walt Disney World executives about the issue was only responded to by the lone woman, Christine McCarthy. You go, Christine!

In the Traditions handbook, we were told in the antiquated vernacular of the times not to be a Petulant Paul, a Bored Bill, a Harried Harriet, or a Sour-Puss Sal. By the 1971 edition, the guys had morphed into Sad Sam and Grouchy Gus. Harriet was retained but not Sal. This came at a time not far removed from when we had been warned in elementary school not to be a Pushy Pig or Grabby Goose. From Mickey and Minnie Mouse to Donald and Daisy Duck to Clarabelle Cow and Horace Horsecollar, alliteration was ever-popular when creating nomenclature. While we tour guides may have felt, on occasion, a bit like Harried Harriet, we would never have thought, under any circumstances, of being deliberately rude to a guest.

Every generation since ancient times, it seems, has bemoaned the manners of the one that came after it. In 1907, Kenneth John Freeman wrote in his Cambridge University dissertation: "The counts of the indictment are luxury, bad manners, contempt for authority, disrespect to elders, and a love for chatter in place of exercise." Although this quote has been erroneously assigned to Plato or Socrates, Freeman is the originator. I knew exactly the kind of people he was describing about over a hundred years ago—those gol-durn young whippersnappers!

Seriously, though, I wanted to personally administer to three Walt Disney World hosts an emphatic remedial lesson in guest relations or at least send them back to the Florida campus of Disney University for additional training. Instead, I just took home, along with all the tremendously cool souvenirs and happy memories, some strongly negative impressions of several cast members. Had these guys really undergone the same kind of training still so clear in my memory?

It is hard to adequately describe the sense of awe I experienced when first walking into Disneyland, or at least into the park's administration building, as a cast member. It was such a tremendous privilege to finally be sitting in a classroom at the University of Disneyland after so many years spent dreaming of this very moment. I could almost swear I heard the faint strains of the "Hallelujah Chorus" playing softly in the background.

Those of us who would begin work over winter break attended orientation and training classes over three consecutive evenings in December. It was an intensive indoctrination into all things Disney, and I loved everything about it. Well, maybe not the "is that your real hair" question, but just about everything else. Soon, we'd go our separate ways to be trained in our own particular areas of expertise, but this was a time to collectively soak up the culture of Disneyland itself and the unique Disney way of doing things. It was a time of such singular excitement, anticipation, and pride. We loved Disneyland, and most of us had grown up with the park, at least those of us from southern California.

The memory of Walt Disney himself was very much a part of the training magic. In the short, instructive videos we watched, he was usually the one talking to us from the screen, just as he had every Sunday night on television for as long as any of us could remember. The oft-repeated, now-famous quotes were simply his inspirational way of speaking.

He shared with us, in that folksy, easy manner of his, just how special and how important each one of our jobs was. Without us, the show couldn't go on. He made us believe that we mattered, that our contributions would be sincerely acknowledged and appreciated. Walt and Roy, along with our peppy University of Disneyland instructors, emphatically conveyed that every one of us had not only the potential but the responsibility to create happiness for other people. In fact, that was the only reason we had been hired. In his insightful book *Window on Main Street* (Theme Park Press, 2015), Van France summed it up perfectly: "Pixie dust is our product."

Tour Guide 101

"Hi, my name's Andrea. I'm eighteen, and I'm a freshman at Occidental College."

Our small training group sat around a conference table, black "leatherette" notebooks open in front of us, pens poised. We took turns introducing ourselves, slightly nervous but also excited. After all, we were being given the metaphorical keys to the kingdom. We wore our beautiful new costumes for the first time, which instantly transformed us from wanna bees into queen bees.

"*Whaa-whaa-whaa-whaa-whaa. WHAA?*"

It was the plummy British accent of Supervisor Cicely Rigdon, but to me, it sounded like the voices of adults on a Charlie Brown cartoon, the ones made by some kind of distorted horn. You knew the off-screen parents or teachers were saying something, you just couldn't understand the words. It was background noise. Like the Charlie Brown gang, we were far more interested in each other, our new costumes, and in the other park cast members, than we were in listening to the voice of an adult.

There were two of us who could speak Spanish, although Peridot could speak it far better than me with the fluency of a native. Her short, dark, natural curls were tucked neatly under the navy velvet riding cap. I'm sure no one had ever asked her if they were real. One girl spoke high school French. The remaining tour guides would only be giving tours in English. Summer training groups would be as much as three times as large as this one.

Coincidentally, one of the new guides came from the same small town as me, although we had attended different schools. She had gone to high school, she said, with handsome Roger Mobley, a Disney child actor. That was pretty impressive, as far as I was concerned. If you were obsessed with horses, you'll remember him as spunky little Packy Lambert on Saturday morning's *Fury*. If you weren't, you might know him as the dashing title character in "The Adventures of Gallegher" on Disney's Sunday night show *The Wonderful World of Color*.

"Oh, yeah, Roger's pretty cool," Tanzanite told me airily. "He was absent a lot with filming."

"I can't believe you actually *know* him!" Could I gush any more pathetically?

As this conversational exchange was going on, I didn't know it, but the young actor was serving a two-year tour of duty in Nam as a Green Beret. He reportedly said of his interrupted cinematic career, "Uncle Walt had plans for me, but so did Uncle Sam, and Uncle Sam won." Roger returned home safely in November 1970.

"Oh, sure," she confirmed. "We went out a couple of times." Tanzanite shrugged casually as though we all dated movie and television stars, didn't we?

Throughout this memoir, by the way, I give the tour guides names of precious gems. From where I sat, they certainly were a glittering, rare, and sparkling collection. When someone is breathtakingly attractive, I always joke that you can't look at them directly or you'll burn your retinas—it's like looking at the sun. Some of the guides honestly were as gorgeous as all that, but in every single case, the most beautiful girls were, without exception, also the most down-to-earth, friendly ones. If I were to tell you their actual names, you would more than likely think I made them up. Their names were as unique and unusual as they were, and for the most part, they were names I'd never even heard before. The names of girls from other countries, of course, were different, but so were those from nearby cities in California. I've often wondered how mothers somehow knew these daughters of theirs could successfully pull off such fanciful, exotic names.

Any former guides who worked at Disneyland from 1969 to 1972 reading this memoir should immediately skip to the Author's Note at the end of the book. The tour guides described in these pages are fictional compilations based on personality traits drawn from many people I knew at the park. If, as Carly Simon sings, "You probably think this song is about you, don't you, don't you?" let me hasten to reassure you that it's not.

Along with the impressive, thick stack of printed materials chronicling just about every bit of Disneyland minutiae, we were given yet another bulletin about THE DISNEYLAND LOOK, as though we might have forgotten what that was since last night. The most important thing we received was our eleven-page-long tour guide spiel. In a couple of days, we needed to commit it to memory. Those of us leading foreign language tours needed to memorize it in two languages. Because no one thought to inform Peridot or me that a copy in Spanish already existed, we also needed to translate the entire document, along with all its Disney-specific vocabulary. We'd be tested on it before we would ever be turned loose in the park with our own tour group. Before that, we'd be assigned to a "big sister" tour guide, a mentor who would show us how it's done in the big leagues.

"*Whaa-whaa-whaa-whaa. Whaa-whaa-whaa-whaa-WHAA!*" Cicely looked pointedly around the table at six upturned faces. Every time she opened her mouth, I was totally unable to focus on the meaning of her words. I found her terribly intimidating.

"*Whaa?*"

She looked directly at me and paused, clearly expecting some kind of a response.

Uh-oh.

"Always use two fingers when pointing—or use your crop," Tanzanite piped up helpfully from the seat next to mine.

Whew.

Usually, I was the teacher's right-hand girl. Yes, okay, pet. Whenever she left the room for a few minutes, I'd be called up to sit at her desk and hold the fort. If there was a play, I was asked to be the teacher. I set up a summer school on my street for the smaller kids. I was a good student and enjoyed school. Here, I simply couldn't relax or concentrate. Frankly, Cicely *always* scared the bejabbers out of me. I'd have to study everything again at home because I certainly wouldn't be able to retain anything that she said to us in class.

There was a green booklet we studied called *Tips to Talkers* with Professor Ludwig Von Drake on the cover holding a microphone. Almost all the literature we received had Disney characters scattered throughout. It made everything seem so official, so "inner circle." *Tips* continued to build on the University of Disneyland's message:

> Remember, YOU are a vital part of the Magic Kingdom. You make buildings, the vehicles, and the streets come alive.

It was true. Without a large staff of loyal cast members on board and fully committed to that message, the park couldn't operate. A great amount of time was being spent training us; we were being well-paid to learn. A substantial financial investment was made before we would ever lead a single tour. Sometimes it worked out, sometimes it didn't: by the time summer rolled around, Tanzanite didn't. Very rarely, guides would be trained and then promptly disappear, never to lead a tour.

Tips to Talkers was absolutely correct about one thing, and that was the importance of caring for your vocal chords. I got in the habit of waiting until people were ready to listen rather than trying to shout over them. That came in handy later when I taught large classes of children and adolescents. If you didn't take care of your voice, you were sunk before your ship set sail. Another requirement was to speak clearly and distinctly, which is always important. If people can't understand you, why are you even talking?

Here are just a few of the oddly enigmatic sentences we practiced to improve our diction:

- Beyond the fund, I was fond of the fun lovers.
- I assume you wish to fume about your doom.
- Since the Prince climbed the fence, he has a pink sink.
- It is your duty to rebuke the spook soon on the dune.
- I wish I could flush a fish from this bush.

Now, honestly, how much do you want to meet the authors and read the rest of the equally pithy epigrams? What fun it must have been at that party—and exactly how much alcohol did the writers consume? They must have been trying to top each other to see who could create the most nonsensical sentence.

"No wait, wait, listen to this one! 'Hurry to the berry patch where Fido will bury his bone.'"

"Ha-ha-ha-hee-hee-hee! Nice one, Joe! Now, please pass me the pretty purple pitcher of pineapple paradise punch. I'm still conscious."

Apart from the spiel, the most critical component of Tour Guide 101 was the yellow-and-orange plaid booklet titled *It's Been My Pleasure*. I could say "my pleasure" without feeling the least bit audio-animatronic, but I would never say the entire phrase. I just couldn't bring myself to do it. The tour guide on the cover was waving good-bye to a man in a suit and tie, a woman in a suit wearing stockings and heels, and a little girl in a dress and mouse ears. Who *were* these people? They certainly never showed up for any of my tours.

The people we'd be taking though the park, our handbook revealed, would be mostly drawn from the ranks of those scared of the California freeways, those who are overwhelmed, people from other countries, people who don't want to miss anything, older folks, people who *always* take tours, people in a hurry, and large families. Sounds like a real fun group, doesn't it? The reality was far nicer. People we encountered on our tours were, by and large, pretty terrific. They were what made doing this job so much fun.

We learned about how to prepare for the tour by first handing out triangular, brightly colored tags to members of our group who would wear them on a string looped around a button or maybe on a purse. We would be doing some friendly, get-acquainted chatting before it was time to leave the Tour Garden. Eye contact was key, but no eye shadow or eye liner! The Disneyland Look was never very far offstage, lurking in the wings. To be fair, eye liner in 1969 meant little tails drawn out to extend past the eyes like those Cleopatra would have recognized.

"Where are you from?" became my standard opening, followed closely by, "Tell me about it." I learned to quickly put people at ease with a genuine smile. A smile was also, in later years, the best way to begin a parent-teacher conference. There was usually some kind of common experience we shared. The guests wanted to know where I went to college, was I just doing this job until I was cast in films (huh?), which places would I recommend they see while visiting in Los Angeles and San Francisco since I lived in both places, and did I have a boyfriend? (Yes, I did.) Nearly all of them were excited and glad to be just exactly where they were. It's hard to go too far wrong when you're dealing with people like that all day, every day. I liked them, and they reciprocated.

We were told to focus solely on our group, a requirement sometimes ignored by pretty, vivacious Tourmaline and a few of the other guides. They sometimes found themselves positively giddy when surrounded by large numbers of good-looking guys who were also working at Disneyland. There was certainly no problem making eye contact in that case.

The tour guide training booklet came to us from the University of Disneyland. The U. of D's familiar crest was featured, but beyond that, the liberal sprinkling of ellipses left little doubt as to the author. Like the famous Z that stands for Zorro, those ... were the distinctive mark of Van France.

We were required to know and deliver our spiel exactly as it was written, but I never knew anyone who actually did that. If that's what the company wanted, guests might as well have carried around those portable, pre-recorded players you see at museums. There'd be no spontaneity at all—just repeating another person's words verbatim day in and day out. We included the main points, of course, followed the same path, and went on the same attractions, but for the sake of sanity, you had to be able to paraphrase a bit and put the facts into common parlance. No one on the planet spoke like the people who wrote the spiel, with the exception, perhaps, of the writers of those sentences in *Tips to Talkers*.

Could *you* say this?

> And now, I hope everyone is ready for the highlight of our train trip. We are about to cross the rim of the Grand Canyon and move back in time to the primeval world. Please don't feed the dinosaurs.

Really? You could? Then how about this?

> And now we're going down Main Street.... By all means watch out for the horses. They still don't like the idea of newfangled cars hogging the street.

You could? Could you say, with a straight face mind you, that those same horses are "paid all the hay they can eat?"

Could you warn your tour group members upon boarding the boats at Pirates:

> Don't be surprised if a pirate jumps into our boat.

I can tell you in all sincerity that *I'd* be pretty darn surprised if it happened—shocked, in fact!

We had to tell our trusting guests that the artificial banyan tree holding the Swiss Family Robinson Treehouse was made using "300,000 hand-painted blossoms and leaves" and that "incidentally, our landscape department calls this species Disney-dendron." The spiel goes on like this for eleven loooong pages. Did I learn it? Yes. Did I ever once say it exactly that way again? What do you think?

Buried under all that yuk-yuk-yuk-it-up brand of broad humor were a good many fascinating facts to share and reminders of appropriate places to stop and talk, to stop and shop, where to take a rest break, and which attractions to point out for guests to enjoy on their own once the tour was finished—or we could simply POINT WITH CROP, as the spiel peremptorily ordered us to do. Someone needed to update and humanize the spiel, and that's what we all did. The bones of it were fine. Like that old dress of Cinderella's mother, however, it needed some beads and maybe a sash to bring it to life.

At last, tedious time spent studying the notebooks around the table with Cicely came to an end. Now, it was time to enter the park and meet the "big sisters" who would continue our training over the next few days.

The very first time the cast door opened from backstage and I stepped through it wearing my tour guide costume was one of the most thrilling feelings I've ever known. The butterflies in my stomach felt as big as those beauties flapping their wings over on the Jungle Cruise. Everything looked like a glittering picture postcard or a Currier and Ives print come to life.

If you have never been to Disneyland during the winter holiday season, you need to book that trip right now. All of the lavish decorations and traditions from a hundred classic Christmas films and holiday television specials will be waiting for you. They go up early and stay late. It never snows, but you won't miss it! Every bit of greenery is flocked with sparkly faux-snow, better than the real thing because it's seventy degrees outside and you don't need to bundle up the kids or wear your mittens.

An impressively tall pine stands grandly in the square on Main Street in front of the train station. The ornaments are gigantic, bowling ball-sized baubles in every color you can imagine, garland and wide ribbons intertwine up and down the entire length of the majestic tree, and on top, an impossibly gorgeous star shines brightly. Oh, and wait until you see it at night! How many twinkling lights of all colors can possibly be twisted around every lamp post and tree? Holly berries, mistletoe, and Christmas bows adorn the tops of doorways. If you've ever wished you could recapture the magical feeling Christmas brought when you were small, you can. It's waiting for you at 1313 Harbor Boulevard in Anaheim, California.

In 1969, local church choirs joined together in a candlelight procession to form a living Christmas tree on the steps of the Main Street train station. The members of each choir dressed in their church's own different colored choir robes beneath white tunics tied with crimson bows. Once the singers took their places and the living tree was finally assembled, it was a moving, poignant sight. Their voices blended in tune with the Disneyland band as they sang the dear old carols. Music rose on the cool night air. Alexandrite, who would be my "big sister" guide, was a part of the tree that year. Everything in the park seemed to sparkle, especially the eyes of those watching.

The Christmas parade was always tremendously popular, too. It usually included those larger-than-life marching soldiers from *Babes in Toyland*, a Disney film starring Annette Funicello and Kevin Corcoran, aka Moochie. There were giant, silly, dancing reindeer with lights strung through their antlers. Some had floppy tongues hanging out; a couple were in immediate need of strabismus surgery. The Disney cartoon and film characters ride along on floats, dressed in their holiday finery. They wave and blow kisses to the guests, and sometimes to the tour guides who line the parade route. Donald gets into the holiday spirit and shakes his tail feathers on occasion. Some of them dance merrily along the streets as sweet strains of Christmas music accompany them. You'll never forget it!

When I thought things at Disneyland could not possibly get any more beautiful, I noticed that the big storefront windows in the Main Street Emporium had been redone featuring miniature, animated winter scenes with Mickey, Minnie, Donald, Daisy, Pluto, Goofy, and popular Disney characters singing carols at a player piano, opening presents, skating on an ice pond, sledding down a hill, and riding in a one-horse open sleigh. Music of the season played softly throughout the entire park. A small group of carolers clad in lavish Victorian costumes looked as if they had stepped right out of a Charles Dickens novel. They strolled slowly throughout the lands, their dulcet voices blending in perfect harmony.

Marveling at the dazzling holiday decorations, the other newest guides and I crossed the square and found the tour guide lounge for the first time. There, we found our big sisters waiting.

"Andrea? Hi, I'm your big sis, Alexandrite." She smiled warmly. Her dark hair was cut in a page boy and curled under to about chin-length. There was a light dusting of freckles across her cute little upturned nose. "You speak Spanish, right?"

"Hi, nice to meet you," I said, smiling back. "Four years high school, half a semester of college."

"Good. I hope we get a Spanish tour this week so you can get an idea of how that goes. Sometimes, it's a little bit harder because you have a tour of half Spanish and half English speakers."

"*What?* Are you *serious*?" I could feel the panic rising already.

"Honestly, it's not that bad. You'll see."

It sounded that bad.

"If you have almost all English and just one or two Spanish speakers, you talk to them as you walk along. Don't worry. You'll get the hang of it."

Surprisingly, I did, but at the time it was hard to believe that any of this would ever feel comfortable. Those of us in our small training group were introduced to the rest of the guides and VIP hostesses who happened to be hanging out in the lounge just then. They were animated, happy, and seemed so confident. Would we be ever be like that?

"Oh my gosh, did you hear, Alex?"

Alexandrite turned to the tall, long-haired guide applying a light coat of lip gloss in the mirror. "Hmm? Hear what?"

"Sapphire and I had our names drawn out of the cap! We get to lead the tour for the USC football team! *Oooooh,*" she squealed, "I just can't *wait!*" She spun around, her long brown curls following a second later. She was smiling and flushed. This sounded like a good thing.

"Lucky you! How fun! Who's leading the Buckeye tours?" my big sister asked.

"Ruby and Turquoise, but I'd much rather lead the USC guys. At least they live in LA. Not much chance of dating a guy from Ohio, is there?"

Alxandrite explained to me later on that every year, members of the two teams playing in the Rose Bowl on New Year's Day were invited to Disneyland and given guided tours. Of course everyone wanted to lead them, so the names of single guides who were full-time were put into a cap and drawn for the honors. The guides were given little embroidered red roses with adhesive on the reverse side. They wore them on their cheekbones. Even after the tours were over, they'd still wear them occasionally, just for fun. All the other girls envied them.

"Alexandrite and Andrea, you two are going out first, right after lunch," Aquamarine told us. She was an experienced dispatcher who knew everything about how the place worked. She was unfailingly kind and helpful.

Not everyone was. A couple of the girls couldn't be bothered to say hello or even look our way. That felt a little like being around an exclusive high school clique. One guide, I later discovered, was a cheerleader at a large, famous California university. I don't ever remember seeing her smile, unless it was when someone else said something mean. She was the rare exception, though.

"Big deal." The cheerleader offered her opinion with a bored yawn. "I see those guys all the time. Believe me, they're nothing special."

"Oh, don't mind her," Alexandrite said. "It'll be *so* much fun!"

A tour guide with the polar opposite personality of the cheerleader's, coincidentally, attended that very same large, famous university. She was the president of the most prestigious sorority in a school loaded to the gills with prestigious sororities. You never saw her without a smile. She greeted everyone warmly, from the people on her tours to the other guides to everyone she met. Hers was a genuine sweetness that couldn't possibly be pretense. You'd recognize her last name because you undoubtedly have several small kitchen appliances that bear the same one. Everyone does. She came to work my first summer and by the next year, she was tour guide royalty, voted tour guide of the year. I frequently saw her name in national business periodicals over the passing decades, and I'm sure everyone who worked with her professionally liked and admired her as much as we all did—well, all of us except maybe the cheerleader.

Being new is never easy, and you need all the help you can get. Luckily, Alexandrite was a pro and knew how to explain everything. She might not have been as glamorous, flashy, and hilarious as a lot of the girls, but she was dependable and didn't have a mean bone in her body. When I was a new teacher, I worked with some people who were helpful and other people who did everything short of outright sabotage. As I gained experience, I decided I'd much rather count myself in the former group.

"We're up. Let's go," Alex said after we had finished lunch at the Pit Stop, a cast-only restaurant located in the tunnels under New Orleans Square. It was the only place where the tunnel system existed in the park. By the time Walt Disney World was built, tunnels ran under Florida's entire Magic Kingdom.

Most of us usually ate at the Pit instead of at the much larger Inn Between behind the Plaza Inn. The Pit was friendly, fast, and good, and was closer to the Tour Garden. Some of the guys tried to scare us by saying there were rats down in the tunnels. I never saw any and don't know if the stories were true or just a (sub)urban legend.

We headed out the lounge door into the Tour Garden. It felt like entering the lion's den, but that feeling quickly lifted as we met our guests.

For the next few days, I would shadow Alexandrite as she gave her tours. I was glad to have someone so relaxed and professional to train me. She wasn't flashy or funny, but she was extremely competent and always took good care of her "people," as we sometimes fondly called our guests. It sounded as though we were a bunch of junior Evitas. You'd hear guides say, "My people were great" or "I gave my people a few extra minutes in New Orleans because they loved it so much" or even "I nearly lost one of my people!" Knowing how to do quick head counts was helpful as a teacher, too. It was like being a mother hen with a flock of distracted chicks, and who could help being distracted at Disneyland?

We did get to do a couple of Spanish tours, which was useful. I saw how appreciative the Latino guests were and was able to chat informally with them individually while Alexandrite led the tour. I learned how to jump in the deep end and converse without being overly worried about making a small mistake. Spanish speakers were exceptionally forgiving.

The day eventually arrived, the day I would lead my own tour! My big sis would accompany me this first time, but I'd be the one giving the spiel and setting the pace. It was a huge moment! Alexandrite had "passed" me on the memorization and said it was time for me to spread my wings.

Here goes. Blue tags, step right this way!

"Good morning, everyone. As you probably already know, my name is Andrea, and I'm going to be your guide through Walt Disney's Magic Kingdom of Disneyland."

They knew my name because I'd just spent the previous ten minutes getting to know them, passing out tags, and visiting with them in the Tour Garden. I told a particularly friendly, well-dressed couple that this was the first time I'd be leading my own tour. They shared my excitement and seemed to be already firmly in my corner.

I gave my introductory remarks standing on the stacked-stone planter just outside the Tour Garden. That spot became notorious one summer when a new guide, so animated and peppy that it was rumored she downed an entire bottle of Geritol every morning, was starting her tour. She didn't watch where she was stepping and fell backwards into the flower bed, landing right on her bottom. The incredible thing was that she never stopped talking, not for a second, or lost her place in the spiel. She kept going, dusted her skirt off, gathered up her people, and headed for the train, still talking.

My opening remarks went without a hitch. I was a little worried about getting the quote on the dedication plaque just right: "Disneyland is dedicated to the ideals, the dreams, and the hard facts that have created America … with the hope it will be a source of joy and inspiration to all the world." Yes, you'll find the ellipsis periods there if you look, but Walt said it, not Van. The small plaque is located by the flagpole. Getting it wrong would have been like mangling the Pledge of Allegiance.

I had done it! Let the games begin.

I confidently raised my riding crop and led my first tour group up the closest ramp leading to the Main Street train station. As soon as I arrived at the top, I noticed with a sinking feeling in my stomach that strong chains were locked around the iron gates and an emphatic EXIT sign was posted. I had led my people straight up the exit ramp.

"Oops, folks, looks like we're going to need to turn around and follow Alexandrite back down the ramp. We need to go up the stairs, not the ramp, to get inside the station." I wish the pavement had opened up and swallowed me whole right then. I'm sure my face was at least as red as my vest.

```
                    TOUR GUIDES

                                    NARRATION-LIVE
                                    Revised October, 1971


.   .   .   .   .   .   .   .   .   .   .   .   .   .   .   .   .   .   .   .   .

    TOUR GARDEN

    GOOD (MORNING, AFTERNOON, EVENING) EVERYONE.  MY NAME IS _____,

    AND I'M GOING TO BE YOUR GUIDE TODAY THROUGH THE SIX AREAS OF

    DISNEYLAND.  IF YOU HAVE ANY QUESTIONS AT ANY TIME, PLEASE FEEL FREE

    TO ASK, AND I'LL DO MY BEST TO ANSWER.  ALSO, IF I'M WALKING TOO

    FAST OR NOT SPEAKING LOUD ENOUGH, BE SURE TO TELL ME.


    I'M SURE YOU'LL BE INTERESTED TO KNOW THAT BEFORE JULY 17, 1954,

    THIS LAND WAS ALL ORANGE GROVES.  THEN THE CONSTRUCTION OF DISNEYLAND

    WAS STARTED . . . THE RESULT OF TWENTY YEARS OF DREAMING BY WALT

    DISNEY AND ABOUT TWO YEARS OF PLANNING WITH HIS CREATIVE STAFF.  OPENING

    DAY WAS ON JULY 17, 1955, EXACTLY ONE YEAR AFTER THE GROUNDBREAKING.

    OUR DEDICATION PLAQUE ON MAIN STREET READS, "DISNEYLAND IS DEDICATED

    TO THE IDEALS, THE DREAMS, AND THE HARD FACTS THAT HAVE CREATED AMERICA

    . . . WITH THE HOPE THAT IT WILL BE A SOURCE OF JOY AND INSPIRATION

    TO ALL THE WORLD."


    THAT WAS WALT DISNEY'S DREAM FOR DISNEYLAND, AND EACH OF THE AREAS WE

    SEE TODAY HAS ITS OWN SPECIAL ROLE IN BRINGING THAT DREAM TO REALITY.

    WE'LL BE VISITING MAIN STREET, ADVENTURELAND, NEW ORLEANS SQUARE,

    FRONTIERLAND, FANTASYLAND, AND TOMORROWLAND.  BUT FIRST, LET'S TAKE

    THE SANTA FE AND DISNEYLAND RAILROAD FOR A GRAND CIRCLE TRIP AROUND

    OUR ENTIRE MAGIC KINGDOM.

    IN FRONT OF TRAIN STATION

    WALT DISNEY ALWAYS HAD A KEEN INTEREST IN STEAM TRAINS . . . IN FACT
```

"Oh, honey, don't worry about it," Anne, the friendly lady standing in front of me said kindly. She was slim and impeccably dressed, wearing gorgeous jewelry that definitely wasn't part of the Disneyland Look. She seemed elderly at the time, but she was probably considerably younger than I am right now.

"That's okay, Andrea," her helpful husband, Bill, added. "We needed the exercise, didn't we, Anne?" he laughed. "Lead on!"

That sweet, silver-haired couple talked to me throughout the tour. They laughed gamely at the feeble jokes from the spiel I scrupulously adhered to with Alexandrite monitoring my delivery. They went out of their way to ask perceptive questions and generally became my new best friends for the next two-and-a-half hours. I couldn't thank them enough for making me feel like a real tour guide and not completely Goofy. After that cringe-worthy start, the remainder of the tour was blissfully smooth, thank goodness. I don't think I could have survived another big blunder.

"Good-bye now, and have a happy day in Walt Disney's Magic Kingdom!" I delivered the very last line in my spiel and waved, a reasonable facsimile of the tour guide pictured on the cover of the *It's Been My Pleasure* handbook.

Anne and Bill gave a couple of spontaneous cheers and led the rest of the guests in giving me a big round of applause. I stood there smiling, blinking back tears, humbled by their thoughtfulness.

Alexandrite commiserated with me back in the tour guide lounge about the unfortunate start to the tour.

"I could see what was happening, but I just couldn't do anything to stop it."

Right, sort of like watching a train wreck.

My doomed Charge of the Light Brigade up the exit ramp was the first but by no means the last time I had to snatch victory from the jaws of defeat. Sometimes, the only thing you can do is keep putting one foot in front of the other. Once, while I was a student teacher standing in an elementary school classroom, seven other adults were also in the room. It made me so nervous I could hardly think straight. There was the cooperating teacher, a sign language interpreter, a social worker, two parents, the principal, and a representative from the Area Education Agency. I was in the midst of giving a spelling test to a class of first and second graders. It was like being on a slide under a microscope. Every last remnant of intellect leaked right out of my ears. The spelling word in question was *an*. I was supposed to say it twice and then use it in a sentence. Unfortunately, I had inadvertently left my brain at home that morning and could not think of a single way to use that common little article.

"Next word. An. An." Pause. Longer pause. "Can anyone think of a way to use 'an' in a sentence?" I asked brightly, looking around the room. Many small hands shot eagerly into the air.

"Austin?" He beamed back at me.

"I see *an* apple."

Oh, Austin, how can I ever thank you? I've learned at times like these to ask for help; you'll almost always find people, especially kids, who are enthusiastic and eager to pitch in.

The winter of 1969 was the first time I ever worked on Christmas Day. As Van had truthfully warned us in the Traditions booklet, "We work while others play." It was true. I wasn't used to the park being so crowded, although I'm sure there was some Disney euphemism for it. Guests packed tightly together like sardines in a tin can, perhaps?

On one of my tours the day after Christmas, it took us twenty-five minutes to cross from the *Mark Twain* dock to the entrance to Frontierland, a short distance which should have taken us five. The area was a writhing mass of humanity. Tours were far longer than usual, queues were longer, and tempers were shorter. It was excellent training, though, because if we could make people happy and show them a great time under those challenging conditions, working on an average day would be a walk in the park!

As winter break was drew to a close, I could look back on my Disneyland training period proudly. I had survived. I was a graduate of the U. of D. and a fully trained tour guide. I'd be ready to start back to work in June with some experience. It felt pretty good. Only a few more days of work, and then it was back to college.

"Andrea, wait a sec. Cicely wants to talk to you." Aquamarine stopped me on my way back from the second tour. I was getting ready to punch out my time card and go home after a very busy, tiring day.

"Do you know why, Aqua?" I tried to act nonchalant, but all of a sudden I had no spit whatsoever left in my mouth. Have you ever had that cotton-mouth feeling when you're really scared? If you have, you'll remember it. It has to do with the physical fight-or-flight response controlled by the autonomic nervous system. I knew which one I'd rather do, and it wasn't fight.

"No idea." Sucking it up, I knocked on the door to her office.

"*Whaa?*" came the muffled invitation to enter her beautifully appointed space.

I poked my head inside. "Aquamarine said you wanted to talk to me?" Just when everything had been going so well, too. Was this the beginning of the end of the shortest tour guide career in park history?

"I wanted to share this with you," she said, beckoning me in with her manicured hand and greeting me with a genuinely warm, friendly smile. I could understand her words! She didn't seem nearly as scary as she had before. "This was sent to me. A couple on your first tour, Anne and Bill, wrote to tell me how well you did and how much they enjoyed spending time with you."

They were from Phoenix, Arizona, and their little telegram-letter had a picture of a cactus and a roadrunner on it. If they'd been standing in front of me just then, I'd have given them a huge group hug. How fantastic could two people be? They'd rescued my tour and now had written to my supervisor telling her how well I had done.

"Yes, I remember them. They were the nicest couple ever!"

"I'll put this into your personnel file. Congratulations. Alexandrite said you did a very nice job during training, too. We'll be looking forward to seeing you back here next summer," she told me.

"Thank you, Cicely. It's been my pleasure."

All right, so maybe I did say it just *once*.

The front cover of an issue of cast member-only Backstage *magazine.*

A Member of the Caste

This chapter is going to sound decidedly elitist, so if that's going to disturb anyone's egalitarian sensibilities, please skip immediately to the next one. No, wait. Better skip on over to Chapter Six to be entirely safe. It honestly can't be helped, because the hierarchy inherent among cast members truly *was* elitist, almost feudal in its rigid, long-standing codes of conduct, and just as in feudal times, Disneyland cast members rarely had much vertical mobility. Most people stayed firmly where they were placed on the day they were cast.

There were positions that represented park royalty (remember, we wore that Royal Stewart tartan), namely tour guides and VIP hostesses, Jungle Boat skippers, the guys at RETLAW, and perhaps a scant handful of others. Next came the aristocracy, bold and handsome knights like the monorail drivers, Matterhorn Bobsled crew, submarine or *Mark Twain* pilots. Then there were the townsfolk, the vast majority of the rest of the ride operators, perfectly respectable, hard-working individuals diligently going about their daily occupations.

Finally, at the margins of our little society were the serfs, legions of busy worker bees, with positions like the sweepers, retail clerks, and food servers. Within each level, however, even further, finely-graded segmentations existed. Okay, so you're in retail. Did you work at the enormous Main Street Emporium or on some little cart stuck on a corner in Fantasyland selling post cards and pencils? You're in food service? Were you a host in the new and decidedly upscale French Market Café in New Orleans Square or did you peddle popcorn from a mobile cart? Operations, huh? Do you load Alice in Wonderland or Autopia? Peter Pan or PeopleMover?

One summer afternoon, I was booking it through Fantasyland's "semi-secret" shortcut gateway, my two-inch heels clicking sharply on the colored pavement, to where I had been assigned the role of area hostess for a few hours. I looked over, surprised, to see a childhood friend of mine stuck behind the counter in some nondescript quick-food place, the Carousel

Corner, wearing a widely striped purple and white blouse that resembled nothing so much as a window awning. There was a tiny pouf of gathered lace pinned precariously atop her head. On what planet is that considered a hat? Sometimes costumes robbed you of any shred of dignity. Longish skirts, shapeless pants. No one took a lot of pride in those costumes. How could they?

It felt as though I had come upon Hans Christian Anderson's Little Match Girl. I swear you could almost hear the bitter Copenhagen winter winds whistling down icy, cobblestoned streets. There was my old friend Judy, fallen upon hard times, grease and mustard stains on her apron-front. She might as well have been wrapped in a shawl standing in ankle-deep snow calling, "Matches! Please, sir, buy my matches."

Veering over to say hello, it dawned on me that I hadn't seen her in maybe seven or eight years. What could we possibly talk about? Math homework? Girl Scouts?

"Hey, Judy, didn't know you worked here. How's it going?"

She swept back a wisp of hair that had managed to escape from the pouf-hat with one hand and gave me a tired smile. Park guests surrounding the counter were hot and tired, three or four deep waiting for their ice cream, hot dogs, hamburgers, Cokes, fries.

"Hi, Andrea. Good to see you. I'm doing fine. Busy, though," she observed, looking from side to side, stating the obvious. "We're always busy." She spread her hands apart, palms up, as if I couldn't see the situation for myself. "You know how it is."

Well no, I didn't, actually. I had no idea what that kind of a job at Disneyland would be like. There was an uncomfortable pause, neither of us finding much to say. It had been a long time since her family had moved away from our little street.

"Okay, well, I'd better get going." I gave a small wave, setting off for some shady corner of the Magic Kingdom to smile and hang out for a bit. The most taxing thing I'd have to do all afternoon would be to tell someone where the rest rooms were located, helpfully labeled Prince and Princess in Fantasyland, or possibly point them in the direction of Small World.

"Yeah. Well, see you around," she said, turning back to her burgers.

I never did see Judy again, but that bittersweet moment has always stuck with me. It was nice to see her after so long, but it was also uncomfortably like seeing an old pal down on her luck, barely making ends meet. That wasn't the case, of course, but that's how it felt at the time. That job didn't look like it was much fun at all.

My cousin Matt, a sweeper, might have held one of the lowest status jobs at Disneyland, but don't get me wrong. Even the lowest man on the Disneyland totem pole, and there *were* some positions even lower than sweeper, was still widely considered by the average college student living in southern California at that time to be a really plum job. Instant social cachet, that's what working in the park gave you. You had a wealth of insider information and access to backstage stories all your friends would envy. Not only that, there was that sweet little Friday night perk called Date Nite at Disneyland, a fond tradition which appears in greater detail in Chapter Nine.

Plus, you worked at the "Happiest Place on Earth." My dad used to say with more than a trace of irony, "Welcome to the Happiest Place on Earth," whenever we visited the park and passed a child howling to the heavens, rivers of tears and nasal discharge running down her face because she had let go of a Mickey Mouse helium balloon, or his ice cream cone had been unceremoniously dropped on the sidewalk, or the poor kid was just plain exhausted. How bad could it be?

Don't forget that by the parsimonious Scrooge McDuck standards of the day, the pay was more than decent. Disneyland paid a lot more than flipping burgers, which is what my boyfriend Ron had done to pay for his college tuition. Working conditions were, for the most part, very pleasant, and extras like an Olympic-sized dating pool full of seriously attractive young people came with the job.

Still, there existed a clear hierarchy of positions within the park, and the uniform you wore put you firmly into a highly stratified caste system even a Brahmin might recognize. For anyone unfamiliar with the term hegemony, it means leadership or dominance, usually by one country or social group over others. In the case of park cast members, we're talking about social group domination. A few synonyms for hegemony are supremacy, dominion, power, sovereignty, and dominance. It's a word perfectly coined to describe what working at Disneyland was like in 1969.

As noted, tour guides and VIP hostesses were perched firmly and unshakably at the top of the cast member totem pole. Maybe it was a self-perpetuating myth, but it was also a widely-accepted one, and frequently observed by cast members of all castes, because it was accurate. Van Arsdale France, founder and Prof. Emeritus of Disney University, puts it this way in his fascinating book *Window on Main Street*:

> A caste system had developed, with some groups feeling like they were far better than others. (And the tour guides felt they were better than everybody.)

Van might have been speaking tongue-in-cheek, but he was absolutely right, we did—and it wasn't just us who felt that way. Everybody at the park acted like the tour guides were better than everybody else, and that is exactly how they treated us. Show me one official picture of cast members taken in those years where a tour guide isn't in the front row, just one.

Our uniforms were seriously gorgeous, beautifully tailored from the finest-quality materials, both imported and domestic. No expense was spared from the tops of our navy velvet riding caps to the red Pendleton woolen socks on our feet. We had a spacious indoor lounge for our exclusive use filled with small, personal lockers, clean rest rooms just for us, couches, chairs, and mirrors (okay, there were *lots* of mirrors). This all might seem relatively ordinary until you did some area hostessing and spent time in other cast members' "break areas."

No air conditioning there. In fact, as Gertrude Stein once observed of the city of Oakland, California, "There is no 'there' there." Some of the "break areas" were just a couple of chairs pulled up to a lopsided table in a sparse little patch of backstage shade. No wonder that kind of favoritism bred resentment! So how did tour guides maintain their social status? I can only say a lot of it had to do with the careful screening process before we were cast, which was tremendously selective. That was coupled with the supreme belief we all held that our job genuinely was the best of the best.

Many years later, as a teacher of adolescents, I noticed that young girls with the most social status currency to spend were, by and large, those with the most unshakable self-confidence. Lots of girls may be far more attractive, kinder, more talented, or smarter than these young social divas, but no one matched them for the supreme belief they held that they were exceptionally special. Maybe it was that way with the tour guides, too. We felt special because we were always treated as though we were. It became something of a self-perpetuating cycle.

Once, long after my tour guide years were but a fond memory, I was teaching an elective drama class. A beautiful girl named Dakota, who was also enrolled in my English class, had to perform her solo monologue on stage. This girl was not popular in the least. She was tall, slim, and perhaps just a bit awkward. Not into sports. Smart enough but not in the "Knowledge Masters" category. The short piece she had been given to perform was about a teenaged girl who was going to show her girlfriend exactly how to get the guy she wanted.

"No, you gotta move like this, Jennifer. It's like the motion of the ocean," she urged her imaginary friend, gently swaying her hips from side to side and moving her hands like some proficient hula dancer just dropped by from the Royal Hawaiian to demonstrate. "That's right, the motion of the ocean."

She was simply stunning! Long black hair, dark sapphire eyes, lithe and lovely in every way. She had casually flipped on a pair of stylish shades for her role and nailed that monologue to the wall. I had seen it done many times before by scores of girls but never so effectively. There was a stunned pause when she finished, closely followed by a roar of spontaneous applause and whoops from the audience of her peers.

Then, she removed the sunglasses and transformed back into the shy, quiet girl we all knew. It was mind-blowing the way she had slipped into the role of that confident character like she was putting on a pair of favorite flats. She was a natural, and I told her so in no uncertain terms in front of the entire class. I don't impress easily, I recognize talent when I see it, and I don't say things I don't mean. When I complement a student, they can be sure that it's absolutely genuine.

"Dakota, you rock! You WERE that girl! I believed every single thing you said. It was as though you were making it all up on the spot. Believe me, you're a star, kiddo, a real star!"

The rest of the students jumped in to add their own accolades. She was glowing.

For the rest of that year, I thought about how young Dakota was really two people, a shy adolescent caterpillar slouching along, ducking her head, unsure of her place in the world. At the same time, just beneath the surface, was that confident, beautiful butterfly poised and ready to fly. I could see the accomplished young lady she would one day become, but she was still wrapping herself in the chrysalis of self-doubt that year.

Much later, I would get an email from her telling me that my confidence in her had not been misplaced. She said how much she appreciated having a chance to shine in drama class that year and what the affirming and positive experience had meant to her. Dakota eventually left Iowa for southern California after she won a scholarship to a well-regarded private college. She was selected as Miss Iowa in one of the famous national scholarship pageants! Not every story, of course, has that kind of happy ending, but I learned while working at Disneyland that being confident about your own abilities can take you pretty far in life.

An accurate description of the Disney cast members' social totem pole during the 1960s may be found in a series of articles written by a former Jungle Boat skipper, now a professor of management and organizational studies at an extremely prestigious, nationally known university. He looks at the park hegemony from a bit more jaded point of view than mine, and you might find his tone just a tad tinged with ax-grinding snarkiness. Once I read the end note in one of his articles about the reason for his being terminated and the ritualistic stripping of his rank, it was easy to understand why he still resents his public demotion from high-status Jungle Boat skipper to unemployed civilian. Yes, the firing process itself was galling, perhaps even gratuitously emphatic, but after receiving repeated warnings about cast dress code violations, specifically his hair length, it could not have been entirely unexpected.

Thinking you can skirt the hair code is like touching the third rail. Don't do it if you don't want to get fried—*and* fired. If you're a girl, your hair can't ever be straight, and it can't be too high. That's why I once got a ruler stuck into my hair before taking out a VIP tour and just managed to limbo under that magic two-inch mark. Men's hair couldn't fall more than midway past the ear. Period. No one could possibly be unaware of the emphasis Disney put on being neatly groomed. The Disneyland Look was very clearly delineated, especially in the 1960s and 70s.

That odd little bump next to the cheek on the inside of the ear, anatomically referred to as the tragus, was the figurative Papal line of Demarcation. Men, grow your hair to that point and no farther or risk termination. Ignore the iron-clad rule at your peril. While moving from Jungle Boat skipper to renowned university professor isn't exactly a step down in the world, it's eminently clear from the tenor of his prose that the long-ago humiliation still rankles to this day.

In fact, the professor has written extensively about The Walt Disney Company's way of doing business, trading on his insider experiences. He even discusses the satisfyingly sweet irony of lecturing on Disney organizational reality, in juxtaposition to the idealized version touted in company literature, at the Anaheim Convention Center adjacent to the park itself. While his observations about the park's social classes very neatly align with my own, it's hard to muster up a lot of sympathy for his being fired for wanting to wear his hair longer than was allowed. That's what we signed up for, after all. Check your individuality at the employee entrance, please.

Most, but by no means all, of the kids who worked at the park were drawn from the densely populated areas immediately surrounding Anaheim in the heart of Orange County—Santa Ana, Buena Park, Cerritos, Fullerton, Garden Grove, and even snooty Newport Beach. Within the ranks of the tour guides, there were also many girls who were from other countries. Since our guests came from all over the world to visit Disneyland, so did the guides who spoke a combined total of some twelve different languages and several dialects at any given time. I worked alongside girls from Egypt, Mexico, France, Germany, Spain, Israel, England, Brazil, the Netherlands, and Japan. It was something of a crash course in international relations.

Being able to speak another language was a distinct advantage. Some of us had taken between four and eight years of a foreign language in school. My Spanish was hardly of the native speaker variety just a few months out of high school, but I could do okay with my trusty spiel memorized.

Ruby, an experienced guide from Mexico, very soon to become a dispatcher, was kind enough to translate some of the trickier words and phrases that didn't appear in my Cassell's Spanish Dictionary:

Mickey Mouse: el ratón Migelito

Horse-drawn street cars: tranvía de caballos

Penny Arcade: arcada del centavo

Sleeping Beauty Castle: el castillo de la Bella Durmiente

Snow White and the Seven Dwarfs: Blanca Nieves y los siete enanitos

Rest stop: parada de descanso

Souvenirs: recuerdos

Haunted Mansion: la casa de las fantasmas

Monorail: el monoríal (I could have maybe guessed that one)

Matterhorn: el matterhorn (yeah, that one, too)

I can say without a hint of exaggeration that the girls chosen to be guides were among the most attractive and personable group of young ladies I have ever encountered in one place before. Being able to take twenty or more strangers through a crowded park and keeping them happy and entertained for several hours wasn't something just anyone could do. The guides learned how to be quick at putting people at ease, to converse with people of all ages about a wide variety of topics, and to speak a different language if that were called for.

The first guys we saw at the start of every tour were the RETLAW train conductors because "a grand circle tour of the Magic Kingdom" was the first thing we did with our guests. The name RETLAW is Walter spelled backwards, and if you know anything at all about Walt Disney, you know about his fondness for trains. It was an entirely separate division from the rest of the park workers. You either worked for Disneyland or for RETLAW. They were an autonomous bunch, not arrogant exactly, but not subject to the rules and regulations of lesser beings. During Walt Disney's time, the RETLAW guys were even invited to his private Christmas party.

They didn't actually drive the big steam engines around the park—that was left to seasoned professional engineers—but they rode along and were always nice to talk to. They were also great to pass along useful information or sometimes gossip from other parts of the park since they looped around so many times a day. They helped us quickly get our groups on and off the passenger cars with a minimum of fuss. I don't know what the job requirements were as stated in the application, but the RETLAW guys I remember were very tall, very tan, very handsome, and usually had dark hair. You rarely saw one alone, and most of the tour guides would happily date someone who worked in RETLAW. In fact, at the tour guide banquet, one of the lines from a song in a humorous skit I recall was: "Don't ask me out unless you're in RETLAW or Operations." It's only funny because it's true.

The Jungle Cruise skippers were also considered top tier. They needed to be personable with their boatload of guests for about ten to twelve minutes. They had to crack jokes while driving the boat. That's not so difficult, considering *Kissimmee Kate* or *Ganges Gal* is on a rail, you don't need to steer, and you have a fairly short spiel to deliver. Originally, the trip down the exotic rivers of the world was more along the lines of a nature documentary, and there were no cringe-worthy puns or jokes at all. In fact, before it was deemed unfeasible, Walt had wanted live animals featured on the cruise. By 1969, when I started working there, however, the animals were realistic facsimiles and the guys had to be genuinely funny and deliver their wise-cracking lines convincingly.

They, like the RETLAW guys, were usually handsome and dashing; they looked like younger, cleaner versions of Humphrey Bogart in *The African Queen*, said to be the inspiration for the attraction. We were told at Disneyland University that the Jungle Cruise had been Walt Disney's favorite ride in the park. I can understand why. It still does a booming business with just a few delightful additions and expansions over the years. It's a classic.

The skippers were for the most part lovable rogues, many of whom took their alter-egos to heart. I found their patter to be a big cut above average. No wonder it was a sought-after position. Even if you did get stuck in one of those long lines waiting to board, the ticket-taker (a skipper himself) would say things like, "Euripides would have enjoyed this cruise, folks. Open up your ticket books and You-Rip-A-De-Es right out and have them ready for me!" In those days, pastel-colored tickets were required to ride an attraction, and the best ones were those requiring E-tickets. The ticket your attraction merited sometimes, but not always, dictated your social status within the cast hierarchy.

There were a lot of romantic, lovesick skippers on those boats, and the guys often called out jokes, inside or otherwise, and engaged in light, flirty banter with passing guides. Our tours rarely took us on the Jungle boats because lines were long and slow-moving, making it difficult to load and unload those boats quickly, but we walked by them twice a day. It was uncanny just how many guides decided that the exit for the Jungle boats was the very best spot in Adventureland to work as an area hostess.

After passing through Adventureland, we did take our guests on Pirates of the Caribbean in New Orleans Square, another high-status cast position. In California, we say care-uh-BEE-un, but in the Midwest and on the East Coast, you almost always hear cuh-RIB-ee-un. The attraction was new and costly. It was considered by many to be the best one in the park. It still is. The pirate crew loading the boats was dressed in swashbuckling attire with lots of swash and a couple of buckles. By the time Pirates opened in March 1967, Disneyland had figured out how to move larger groups of people rapidly through an attraction, a problem that continued to plague the Jungle boats and the submarines. Enter on one side, exit on the other, assign rows in advance, and keep it all moving as fast as possible.

This all occurred long before Johnny Depp had appeared on the horizon, me hearties. After sitting through the ride many hundreds of times, I'm sure I was not the only tour guide to appreciate Mr. Depp's exceptionally clear enunciation of the lyrics, "We're devils and black sheep, really bad eggs," in the first Pirates film. Most of us continually wondered in what sense, exactly, could those pirates be considered "jolly-fried-eggs." I, personally, am forever grateful to Captain Jack Sparrow for clearing up that enigmatic eggs reference once and for all.

The cream of the crop: Disneyland tour guides

Caste Aristrocracy ... and the Rest

In the cast of *Gilligan's Island*, there were the more well-known passengers aboard that three-hour tour aboard the *S.S. Minnow* who were designated by generic titles like the millionaire or the movie star, and then there were some euphemistically known as "the rest," lumped together as also-rans. That changed, of course, in later seasons, probably due to some strenuous protests from the Professor and Mary Ann. It was like that in the park as well. There were the attractions operators and then there were the sweepers, the parking lot attendants (right, it was a surprisingly elevated role in 1969) and then there were the balloon peddlers. So first, let's consider the elevated strata of caste aristocracy, and then we'll take a look at "the rest."

Among the remaining members of the caste who could legitimately be called park aristocracy were several other relatively high-status roles. These included:

The coed team of good-looking Matterhorn bobsled operators who were always frightfully busy, due to the ride's enduring popularity. They formed their own exclusive club. They had to cope with some of the longest, rowdiest lines in the park, and it wasn't easy shoehorning four guests at a time in and out of those streamlined bobsleds. Think Tyrolean hats, intricate thread-worked hearts-and-flowers designs on white shirts, and pretty flared skirts or tailored trousers.

Additionally, several guys were hired to actually climb the park's Matterhorn mountain a couple of times a day, inspired by Disney's 1959 *Third Man on the Mountain* film featuring Janet Munro and James MacArthur. That's the same year Disneyland's own 1/100th scale Matterhorn was opened. I can remember the excitement of watching it being constructed and then seeing it become a landmark fixture on the Santa Ana Freeway. The trio scaling our mountain wore lederhosen, which had the potential to produce some seriously major-league wedgies.

The handsome military unit of all-male submarine pilots on their voyage "through liquid space" under the Polar ice cap were also impressive. It's been observed by generations of women from Jane Austen to Debra Winger that there is just something about a man in uniform, and those crisp, navy whites looked pretty darned impressive. They also wore white caps with shiny black bills and looked every inch the naval officers they were portraying. Our daughter, Liz, would be one of the first women to break the gender barrier and pilot a Disneyland sub herself, but that bold advance wouldn't come until more than a quarter of a century later.

The monorail drivers and just about anyone working in Tomorrowland donned sleek, flattering, military-looking uniforms in attractive bright colors. This was before the days of Space Mountain with its own brand of futuristic silver-chic. In the earlier days of the park, a couple of tall, striking space cadets could usually be seen walking around Tomorrowland wearing what looked to be silver lamé jumpsuits with large plastic fish bowl helmets over their heads. Silver always showed up in attire-of-the-future in those days. Fish bowls, not so much.

The *Mark Twain* pilots were clones of the RETLAW guys—typically tall, dark, and always handsome. Did those jobs come with a coupon for free plastic surgery? There was a suspiciously high number of cleft chins and deep dimples among the rank and file. Their costumes consisted of black pants and vests, with crisp white shirts and dark ties, and they wore jaunty caps like those worn by Mississippi river pilots in the 1800s. We took our tours aboard the *Mark Twain* until Bear Country opened in 1972, and after that it was our go-to when one of the regular attractions we routinely visited on our tour was down. It happened from time to time, either due to mechanical breakdowns or seasonal maintenance.

It was fun to choose a likable boy or girl from the guests and take him or her way up to the wheelhouse of the big boat so they could "drive" it down the Rivers of America. There was a guest book to sign and the child came back with a certificate stating they were now officially licensed as a Disneyland riverboat pilot. Mark Twain himself would have enjoyed it! Also, just below the wheelhouse was a small lounge with two facing sofas where a tired tour guide could lie down and occasionally steal a few minutes of rest when things were especially hot or frenetic in the Magic Kingdom. If you inadvertently happened to fall asleep, the pilots would wake you up in time to meet your departing guests on the lower deck.

Years later, when I took my own young children aboard the *Mark*, I asked one of the pilots if it were still possible to visit the wheelhouse. He gladly took us up with him to the wooden door marked PRIVATE. It's a phenomenal vantage point from which to see the park, and little ones have no idea that the beautiful white steamboat is actually riding on a track under the water. When they turn the huge, wooden wheel and the ponderous bow turns right along with it, they are thrilled.

The final high-status position might come as a bit of a surprise. The true mavericks of the park, the real wild cards, were the parking lot attendants. It's true. You'd think people who never get inside the berm might have been considered outsiders. No, the parking lot jockeys were a law unto themselves. They worked the Disneyland gate on Harbor Boulevard, directed streams of cars pulling in from across the country where to park, and corralled the many tour buses into one area. They also were responsible for driving the trolleys full of eager, energetic guests up to the main gate in the morning and the trolleys full of sated, exhausted guests back to where their cars were parked at night. Through it all, they were hilarious, light-hearted, and extremely competent.

They might never get beyond the main gate except on Date Nite, but they gave the distinct impression that they wouldn't trade their freewheeling brand of freedom for any other job in the park. They wore some bright, highly visible color combination of orange and yellow, nothing fancy, but they wore those costumes with utter panache. They were among the genuinely funniest groups in the cast, but they mostly played just with each other. It was another very exclusive club like the Matterhorn gang.

One rainy night in 1963, as my family was leaving the park, we neglected to pay attention to where we were parked, a mistake you can be sure we never made again. We had taken an exchange student from Mexico with us to see the first audio-animatronic show at Disneyland, the Enchanted Tiki Room, still one of my all-time nostalgic favorites. We finally had to throw ourselves on the mercy of the parking lot attendants. That's when I fully appreciated how great they really were.

No complaints, no jokes, as one of their number patiently drove us on some nimble little golf cart-like vehicle up and down practically every row of the entire parking lot in the dark and the rain looking for my aunt's land yacht of a Plymouth Bonneville. The parking lot attendants were everyone's favorite bad boys and girls among the cast, living life on the edge, the lovable black sheep of the Disneyland family. They might be a wild bunch, but you had to recognize and respect the skills.

So those were the rest of the stand-out roles that carried with them a lot of social clout back in 1969 when I became a member of the caste.

The next tier of people working in Operations, the happy crowd of hard-working villagers, was filled with largely interchangeable positions. Don't get me wrong. They still had definite status, but remember, everything was on a sliding scale. If Tomorrowland had the sharpest, most stylish of the Operations costumes, those assigned to Fantasyland had perhaps the dorkiest of them all. It was so definitely a kiddie kingdom, practically untouched since 1955, that it just wasn't a particularly cool place to be. If you loaded Dumbo, Peter Pan, Mr. Toad's Wild Ride (Ron and I loved that one; I was sorry to see it go, but very relieved to find it was simply being expanded and remodeled), the Teacups, Snow White (years before they had to add "Scary" to the title), Alice, or the Carousel, you usually wore some kind of generic white shirt, maybe a pair of Alpine-looking suspenders, plain-colored skirt or pants, and sometimes an overly large bow stuck somewhere on your person.

The only true notables among the majority of the Fantasyland female crowd were the darling Storybook Land girls whose boats were regularly swallowed by Monstro the Whale. They had super-cute, little-girl-style flouncy dresses in pretty shades of pastel with sashes, white aprons, knee socks, and shiny Mary Janes. They were candy-box pretty, and as a group, they were simply adorable. One, in particular, had impossibly long, lovely hair that reached all the way down her back to her knees, and that hair had to be curled every morning!

"Linda Lee?" I asked one of the Storybook Land girls one afternoon as we both happened to be walking through the park at the end of our shifts. I knew it had to be her. The blonde curls were a giveaway.

"Yes, it's me. Andrea?"

"Yep."

"I didn't you know worked here!"

"Same here!"

Notice a familiar pattern emerging in these conversations with old friends?

And as usually happened, I never bumped into her again, but I did think the casting director had certainly hit the nail on the head putting Linda Lee on the boats. She still had the sweetest, dimpled smile and the most impossibly bright, golden curls I remembered from our days together on the pom-pom drill team back in high school. When I say her curls were "impossibly bright," I don't mean to say the color wasn't natural. It was. It was an amazing shade of true blonde that you don't often see. That's how I recognized her. She looked as if she had just stepped out of a fairy tale herself, as delightful as I remembered her, and a perfect candidate for selling, I mean *telling*, those Storybook Land fairy tales to the little ones.

In the small cadre of Fantasyland high-status jobs, you would certainly have to count the Small World attraction operators. I always found their costumes to be especially undignified. Yet, due to its exalted position during the World's Fair of 1964–1965 and E-ticket ranking, it was and remains popular, hence higher status. International visitors, especially, practically jump out of their seats when they spot their homeland being dramatized by small, singing dolls. The welcome and good-bye signs written in many languages are an especially heartwarming touch, and I can testify to the fact that it is very much appreciated. I've witnessed tears on many occasions while riding this attraction, the good kind of tears.

Small World was always the last stop on our tour, and the guests just ate it up with a spoon. The operators on Small World were dressed as Italian gondoliers in red, white, and navy blue with striped shirts and flat straw hats tied with wide ribbons around the crown which trailed down their backs.

When I told my son-in-law, Amos, recently about my jaded opinion of his old Small World costume, he said, confidently paraphrasing Will Smith in *Men in Black*, "Hey, I made that look *good!*" I suppose that's right because he eventually married my daughter who was a sub pilot at the time they met.

The Haunted Mansion in New Orleans Square had just opened in 1969, and while the costumes there were fancy, intricately detailed, and beautifully designed, they were decidedly dark and kind of creepy. It was another E-ticket attraction and immensely popular, so working there was considered a decent assignment.

The generic Old West costumes in Frontierland and Bear Country were okay but nothing out of the ordinary. They were a little too rugged, too *yee-haw*, and too gol' durn mountain man to be highly desirable. They weren't especially flattering to the men, let alone the ladies. If any costume could deduct ten IQ points right off the top, those could.

Leaving the last of the exalted attractions operators behind, and keeping in mind that anything in Operations wasn't bad at all, you'd find those poor, unfortunate souls, "the rest" of the employees who made up the vast wasteland of comparatively low-status cast positions like the sweepers, retail, and food service workers, and I would rank them in that order, from most appealing to least. The sweepers wore nondescript, fairly baggy white pants and shirts, and they pushed trash cans around all day. If you've ever heard the phrase "title tells all," then you have a very good idea of what the sweepers did.

Even so, they were able to be out and about roaming their designated areas at will. If they wandered into an adjacent land, most people wouldn't object or even notice. (The area supervisors would, however, so it wasn't advisable.) They, like the guides, could really go anywhere without seeming out of place. And our guests loved that Disneyland was kept perennially pristine. They positively gushed about it, so the sweepers got some well-deserved props for keeping it that way. Cleanliness was one of the guiding principles in park management back then, and it still is. Walt wanted nothing that even remotely resembled the seedy carnivals or grimy amusement parks that had existed prior to Disneyland.

As far as I could see, most of the food service and retail workers were not especially happy about their positions. Who would be? You come in for an interview hoping to wear the dashing Jungle Cruise costume or that of the sleekly-tailored RETLAW train conductor, and you leave wearing something that more closely resembles a window awning with a big bow pinned under your chin. You're on your feet selling popcorn or balloons all day in the hot sun. Fun? Possibly, at least at first, but it was most assuredly not as fun as many other positions available in the park. Selling frozen bananas from a refrigerated push cart wasn't as appealing as working for seriously good tips in the air-conditioned Blue Bayou or the beautifully exotic Polynesian Terrace. Girls only, though, got those sweet and lucrative assignments.

Retail is basically retail no matter where it's done, and retail in the park comes with its own set of peculiar challenges: crying kids, harried moms and dads, outraged guests who demand a particular souvenir that hasn't been produced since 1957. Why not work at the mall where those challenges wouldn't occur? There had to be some appealing aspects to those kinds of jobs, but if you had to choose a place to work at Disneyland, they would not have been most people's first pick. No way.

Still, regardless of any inherent role status, the park was a wonderful place to meet people, and Disney University went out of its way to create a lot of fun cast activities for socializing, so there was always that.

There is one more, small sliver of a group of extremely select employees I haven't mentioned, and most people will never get a chance to even catch a glimpse of them. They stand outside the berm of regular Disneyland society, a class apart. They are the lovely ladies of Club 33, that private club that actually serves—*shhhhh*—alcohol in the park. As you disembark from Pirates, look to your left and you may notice the very discreet little button next to the 33, for 33 Royal Street, on an otherwise unmarked, unremarkable door. That's all you'll see.

Press it at your peril! Only those on the list are buzzed through to take either the swirling staircase or a quaint, old-fashioned lift to the second floor. The Club 33 waitresses were dressed back then as naughty (or as naughty as Disney girls ever got) French maids. You could practically hear them squeal *ooo-la-la* or *vive la France* as they tottered through the park in the morning on their way to work wearing heels so high no other girl would even think about smuggling them past Wardrobe. These gorgeous young ladies were usually a little bit older than the rest of us part-time employees, and they definitely seemed a lot more worldly. I don't know what kind of tips they made, but I'm sure they must have cleaned up, especially at those Orange County businessmen lunches—and not with those little feather dusters, either.

One day, as I took a VIP tour to lunch at the Club 33, I pressed the button and was happily surprised to find yet another familiar face from my past behind the reception desk checking our names against those on her list.

It was Meg, an old friend from school. Her mother had been our assistant troop leader in Girl Scouts. We had graduated from high school together, but we hadn't seen each other in quite awhile. Meg was always sharp as a tack. She skipped third grade back when that was still done and was very friendly. She didn't wear the French maid costume of the waitresses. Hers was a gorgeous, long black velvet skirt with eye-catching, leg-of-mutton sleeves on a white fitted blouse. Maybe a cameo? A small black ribbon was tied prettily around her throat. I'm sure she must have seen just about every celebrity who visited the park, but there wasn't time to chat, and, as with so many other old girlfriends from school, I never did encounter her again.

In case you're thinking of joining the oh-so-exclusive Club 33, don't hold your breath. The waiting list is currently closed. If it does open up again, however, be sure you have the $25,000 initiation fee per person and the $12,000 annual dues per person on hand. All that substantial investment really gets you is admission to the park and to Club 33, along with six FastPasses instead of the normal three available at no charge to the general public. Once you get in, however, you'll still need to purchase everything on the pricey club menu, and believe me, it's all delicious. Oh, and don't forget to leave your waitress a generous tip!

There were a lot of cool, exciting jobs at Disneyland, that's for sure. Still, I wouldn't trade being a tour guide for anything. I've said if before, but it bears repeating: tour guide was, hands down, the best part-time gig in the park. We spent our time showing people how to most effectively utilize their day at Disneyland and letting them in on some fun "insider" secrets like these:

- As you leave tonight, look above the fire station on Main Street, and you may notice a light burning in the window upstairs. That was Walt's own private apartment and a light is left on in his memory.

- Yes, there really is a small basketball half-court complete with regulation-height hoop inside the Matterhorn, and cast members really do play basketball up there, mostly to kill time as they're waiting to launch Tinker Bell during the fireworks.

- Look carefully at the wrought iron balustrade around the second story above the entrance to Pirates. Can you see the initials WD and RD, their letters intertwined? That was a second private apartment in the park, originally intended for the Disney brothers.

- The first Tinker Bell, Tiny Kline, who flew down from the top of the Matterhorn every night before the fireworks, was a retired circus performer, a spry septuagenarian, who hit smack into a mattress tied around one of the pine trees in a remote area of Fantasyland at the end of her flight.

In the days prior to the internet, before every bit of information has become accessible, some of it true and some not, hearing a little of the inside story on a tour was exciting.

Working as a guide meant decent pay for the times, and we were given awesomely pretty costumes. We spent the day showing people a special place we were proud of and one we loved. We met and worked with wonderful colleagues from all over the world, and we had the freedom to move about the park with few restrictions. Being a tour guide at Disneyland in its early years truly was the best of times. It might sound disingenuous to say we were paid for having fun, but most times that's exactly how it felt to me.

More Disneyland tour guides than you can shake a riding crop at.
Andrea is second down from the upper left, caught in mid-spiel.

Character Sketches and Sketchy Characters

When I started to work, there were some six thousand members of the Disneyland cast, about half of whom worked seasonally like me. There was also a large contingent of permanent full-time employees who made lifetime careers out of working at the park.

Almost all of the children who came to Disneyland, and a surprising number of the teens and adults, too, loved running into the costumed characters strolling about the grounds. These characters usually had assigned places to hang out, but there might have been a bit of flexibility, too. The biggest stars who not coincidentally drew the biggest crowds were Mickey, Minnie, Donald, Daisy, Pluto, and Goofy. Main Street is where you could usually find them. Lots of long lines for hugs and photos, but not very many of those time-consuming autograph books that you see so much of today.

I sometimes hear parents or grandparents say they are waiting to take the little ones to Disneyland or Walt Disney World until they are "old enough to remember it." I have some advice for them. Go now. Go while they are still young enough to believe. The small window of time when your child believes that the strolling Pooh Bear with a "hunny pot" sitting on his head is *really* Winnie goes by in the blink of an eye. Kissing Pluto probably won't appeal much to your twelve year old, but when our daughter was two and a half, she giggled and wriggled with delight as she kissed the silly old dog's long, red rubber tongue. That Pluto was more than five feet tall and walked on his hind legs troubled her not at all. Since you'll see it through your child's eyes, it will be magical for you, as well. Don't miss it!

Working as a character paid very well in the late 1960s and early 1970s. They made perhaps four or five times what tour guides made per hour, and most of them were full time. They earned every penny! They had great working hours, a necessity with the heat as scorching as it was in Anaheim during the summer months. I seem to remember them working with the guests for fifteen minutes, then waving gaily and quickly ducking out the cast back-door to the break area for fifteen minutes off, but that's just a guess on my part. According to my friend who was a Walt Disney World character a number of years after I worked at Disneyland, her time in the chipmunk suit was forty-five minutes on, fifteen off. No matter how long they were confined, it was by no means an easy job.

They removed those large, sweltering heads, as much of the body as was decent, and would sit around chatting with each other, maybe having a much-needed drink to replace all the fluid they lost in those sweat boxes they wore. One afternoon as I was leaving work by the Main Street cast door to punch out my time card, I remember seeing Mickey Mouse, Donald, and Daisy Duck sitting at a backstage table in the shade. The little rodent had on his red shorts while the two quackers wore just their feathered duck-tails. They all wore sweat-soaked, striped T-Shirts and suspenders that held up their lower halves. Three giant heads smiled vacantly from an adjacent table.

In those days, characters that size were usually played by little people, the ones who played Munchkins so effectively in *The Wizard of Oz*. So there sat three middle aged little men, each with a stubble of beard, Mickey balding and smoking a cigar, just shooting the breeze. Mickey Mouse was usually portrayed from 1961 to 1986 by Paul Castle, but to maintain the illusion that Mickey was real, Paul's contributions were seldom acknowledged. Under the table were tucked two pair of adorable orange duck legs and feet, one of the waterfowl duo wearing a satin skirt to cloak her nether regions, the other *au naturel*, and also tucked under were Paul's pair of tiny mouse legs wearing oversized shoes. It was a rare sight to behold, and one that would have sent small children running in the opposite direction, screaming in terror. Mickey Mouse is a little man? Puffing on a stogie? Balding? Seriously, it was the stuff of nightmares.

It seemed that some of the more villainous of the characters on parade in the park had been typecast. They acted up a bit because, hey, they were only doing it "in character." We heard guests complain from time to time that one of the villains had rather badly twisted their child's hand when shaking it, or another had stomped on a foot, or a third had spoiled a photo in the days before digital at the last second by covering the child's face with their overly large paw. At least some of those reports were probably true, and at least in some cases, the little dumplings might have had it coming.

Kids, *big* kids, kids certainly big enough to know better, would harass the poor people encased in those hot, sweaty costumes unmercifully. That's the reason you usually see them accompanied by a character like Alice or Snow White or Mowgli, someone who can protect them and drive off anyone who gets too intent on inflicting harm. Just check out Br'er Bear, Eyore, or Tigger. Most of them have tails that have been pulled off and sewn back on so many times you can see the repair jobs plainly. They'd been swiftly kicked in the rear-end plenty, too. And we saw for ourselves the bruises on some of the characters' legs in the locker rooms—not Daisy, however, as "she" would have been using the men's lockers. Minnie, too.

One summer on a not-too-busy afternoon, I was assigned to area hostess in Fantasyland. After the requisite number of forty-five "on-duty" minutes, I took a break and found Pinocchio sitting cross-legged in a chair, his severed head grinning wildly at me on the table beside him.

"Boy, you got a small waist there," he said companionably. "What, twenty-five inches?"

You, too, I could have accurately observed, have a small waist, sir.

"How's it goin'?" He was a small, dark haired, nice-looking guy, maybe thirty or thereabouts, taking his fifteen minutes off.

"Fine. Not much happening."

"Well, *I* just had somethin' happenin'," he told me with a smile nearly as big as that of his alter-ego.

"Oh, yeah? What?"

"So there's this kid, right? Not some little guy. He musta been maybe thirteen, fourteen years old. And he keeps comin' at me, kicking me, punchin' me, and then runnin' away like a little punk."

"That's too bad. I know how they can be at that age, especially if there're more than one of them."

Kids didn't bother guides, as a rule, but they could be really rough on characters if they thought they could get away with it. Hence, the need for security officers on duty.

"No, this was just one, but he was a real piece of work. He kept comin' back. He'd kick me and then run. Kick and run. See?"

I saw. Unfortunately, I'd seen it happen all too frequently.

"So what happened? Did you call Security?"

I would have.

"Nah." The macho puppet pooh-poohed the idea. "Took care of it myself. I walked over to the tunnel, real slow and easy, back past the clock shop where nobody hardly never goes."

I knew it well. It was the shortcut I'd taken when I had run into my old friend Judy working quick-food in Fantasyland.

"Yeah. Then what?"

Okay, this was getting pretty interesting, now.

"So he spots me there and comes over again, just like I knew he would. I move behind the big stone pillar, back by the bushes, and there's nobody around. Nobody but us."

"What did you do?"

I *really* wanted to know by this time.

I could just envision the big kid, shocked beyond words, manhandled by gentle, harmless Pinocchio who, up until this point, had been a sort of living, smiling punching bag. The tables were turned. The previously hapless puppet-boy now thrust his big happy face, grinning maniacally while wearing a jaunty, yellow hat with perky little feather, toward the boy while gripping him by the throat and shoving him roughly up against the unforgiving stone wall.

"I grabbed that little sucker by his collar, shoved him up against the castle wall, and I says to him, 'Look, kid, get the *HELL* out of Fantasyland and don't you *NEVER* come back! You hear me?' You oughta see that kid run! Oh, yeah, he was runnin' then, for sure—and he's not gonna come back any time soon, neither!"

Of that, I had no doubt.

Get the *HELL* out of Fantasyland? I know I certainly would have. It made you almost feel sorry for the kid. Almost.

We seldom saw the ranch hands at the Circle D Ranch located adjacent to the park who managed the horses and other live animals. There was a lot more livestock than there is now: a big team of pack mules, the large draft horses, Clydesdales, Shires, Belgians, or Percherons, responsible for pulling the trolleys up and down Main Street, shiny-coated Hackney ponies with bobbed tails harnessed to carriages, and lovely white horses, always impeccably groomed, who pulled a fire truck through Town Square back in the park's earliest days.

I've always loved horses and enjoyed seeing them in Disneyland, but I'm sure liability insurance premiums and the mess they leave behind must have contributed to their gradual disappearance in the park. For the most part, just the draft horses remain a regular fixture, with maybe the occasional flashy white horse pulling Cinderella's carriage in a wedding or parade. There have always been a small number of men hired solely for the purpose of sweeping up after the horses. They're called "white wings," just like they were at the turn of the last century in small towns across America, and they push big cans labeled DSD for Disney Sanitation Department.

The landscapers, a substantially larger group, mostly worked hours when the park was closed to the public. Once in a while, if you had an especially early shift, you might see some of them putting the finishing touches on their gorgeous floral creations or trimming those intricate, eye-catching topiaries over at Small World, but for most of us they were invisible, just as in the old elves and the shoemaker story. You saw the results of their incredible handiwork in the morning, but you rarely caught a glimpse of them at work.

One day, you might go home having seen lavish swirls of purple pansies and yellow marigolds in the raised beds lining the walkway leading to

Tomorrowland. The next day, as if by magic, those had been removed only to be replaced with dramatic, candy-striped rows of red and white poinsettias. Our guests from other counties, especially those with growing conditions like Anaheim's Mediterranean climate, always enjoyed identifying and pointing out plants and flowers they recognized from their homelands.

"Andrea, are those bottlebrush bushes?" a friendly Aussie asked me, pointing at some shrubbery with red flowers that did, indeed, look like bottle brushes. Our steam train chugged past Tomorrowland station on our journey to the Primeval World "back when dinosaurs roamed the earth."

"Yes, they are! We have one of them in my backyard at home, too!"

If you visit Disneyland today, you can take a tour designed specifically to answer questions like that. It's cleverly called Cultivating the Magic, and it is led by—who else—tour guides, but now it's a co-ed contingent.

Bill (or Morgan, as he was known) Evans and his brother Jack were responsible for the original park landscaping design. The brothers had successfully landscaped the new Disney family home in Holmby Hills in 1952, and that included the famous Carolwood Pacific miniature railroad featuring the original *Lilly Belle* steam engine. Walt brought them on board in 1954 to do the same thing for Disneyland, albeit on a much grander scale. The brothers were a natural choice and left a lasting, living imprint on the park. The landscaping they put in place sixty years ago continues to grow more beautiful with the passing years.

The Adventureland Jungle was created in under a year, incorporating some existing plants and trees with new ones. It backed up to the Tour Garden, and we could hear the restless cries of wild animals and angry head hunters—"two of his for one of yours"—wafting on the summer breezes. By all accounts, so could the Disney family. The little outdoor patio adjoining their private apartment above the fire station was very close to the back door of our tour guide lounge.

Most of the original orange trees (including ten acres of a grove owned by the Dominguez family; young Ron Dominguez would later become a Disney executive) covering the site where Disneyland was built were long gone. The driver of a bulldozer hired to remove the unwanted ones turned out to be red-green color blind like about eight percent of the male population. He mowed down those orange trees marked red, which were supposed to go, right along with those marked green, which were not. You might still catch a glimpse of one of the very few original ones left or maybe one planted from seeds saved from the old trees.

Another venerable survivor of those ranch days, a giant Canary Island palm tree planted in 1896, graces Adventureland near the Indiana Jones attraction. The elder Mr. Dominguez, Ron's father, specifically asked Walt if it might be saved. It had witnessed so much of his family's history. It could, but the giant had to be balled and burlapped and trucked from its site that became the parking lot to its current spot near the exit to the Jungle Cruise.

Other trees getting a new lease on life were four big fig trees from Pershing Square in Los Angeles. That area was slated for demolition, but resourceful Disney landscapers swooped in to rescue the fig trees. They were carefully removed and driven down the Santa Ana Freeway where they took root in what eventually became New Orleans Square.

The same elves and the shoemaker principle held true for the maintenance guys, and it *was* mostly guys in 1969. If paint were chipped or a light bulb burned out, you can be sure that the next morning it would be taken care of in short order with no trace left behind of the men who had worked so diligently in the wee hours. Plumbers, electricians, carpenters—every trade imaginable was represented. There were legions of park workers who labored all night long to maintain the illusion of perfection. They serviced the vehicles, fixed the enormous amount of moving parts that could break or simply wear out, and kept those audio-animatronic hordes animated.

A group we did see daily, but one you might not even notice when you visit the park, is the security officers. They don't try to stand out, they try to blend in. On Main Street, they might look like your favorite 1900s-style Keystone cop. In Frontierland, they might be wearing a buckskin-fringed vest, a star, and a Stetson hat. Adventureland, New Orleans and Bear County, Tomorrowland, and Fantasyland all had guys (right again, just guys) there to help out if and when they were needed. They rarely were, which is a testament to the good behavior practiced by most of our guests most of the time. By 1969, the security costumes we saw in the park were more of the *Paul Blart, Mall Cop* variety—that is to say, fairly bland. Shades of light blue on dark blue, white military-style officer hats, and white belts and shoes were characteristic. A lot of guys wore white belts with white shoes in 1969, and not just at Disneyland.

They were older than most of the part-time crowd. Some were teachers working their spring, summer, and winter breaks. Others, like sweet, smiling Ray on Main Street, had been on the beat ever since the park opened. They were friendly, might nod at us as we passed by, riding crop held high with a red or yellow or green triangle tag attached so our group could pick us out of the crowd, but they didn't call attention to themselves. They had on unobtrusive headphones so that they could receive or transmit messages, but other than that, you wouldn't notice them. That's the way Walt Disney wanted it. He never wanted guests to feel like they were under scrutiny, but you could rest assured that the security officers on patrol were there to step in and help whenever they were needed.

Management was a constant, quiet part of our small world, too. Like security, they didn't stand out, but there were always a few of them around.

Sometimes, just to say hello, they'd come by the Tour Garden, an out-of-the-way oasis behind the reception desk where tour guests would wait for their tour to begin in a shady green area perched on white, wrought-iron seats. Men who held leadership positions of great responsibility within the ranks of the Disney company were friendly, kind, and unprepossessing. Maybe that was a lesson they learned from Walt himself. There wasn't any feeling of being covertly evaluated or watched, although that must have always been going on to some extent.

You'd be hard-pressed to find a nicer, more laid-back, pleasanter team to work for than those early leaders of Disneyland. The ones I remember fondly as being being most highly visible and always engaged with members of the cast, regardless of which position you held, were Dick Nunis, Ron Dominguez, and Jim Cora. The fact that they started at the bottom of the cast totem pole and worked their way up might have had something to do with it. Management executives were on an entirely different totem pole, naturally, from the one we part-time cast members were.

All of these great men experienced a tremendous amount of well-deserved success. The cream usually rose to the top at Disney, and nice guys finished first. Just because you wield a great deal of power doesn't mean you have to go on a power trip, and none of this group did. Treating those who work under you with consideration is a valuable skill, and their tremendous collective achievements should be an object lesson to managers everywhere.

While many different kinds of characters worked at the park, none were quite as memorable for me as the naughty little puppet boy Pinocchio. Over the course of the summer of 1969, Pinocchio and I got to know each other better. He had been a jockey in Mexico in his youth, and now was happy to have a good, steady job at Disneyland where the only danger was being attacked by junior high school bullies, most of whom he could handle with one wooden hand tied behind his back. Once, he surprised me with this little tidbit of information.

"Lemme see that crop ya got there, Andrea."

"Okay, here you go."

My riding crop, the very symbol of the tour guide, was dutifully placed in his open palm.

He turned it over appraisingly in his small hands and handed it back.

"When I was ridin' races down in Mexico, we used whips, but ours was made from the penis of a bull. Yeah, we used a bull's pizzle. They're real tough. You stretch the skin of it over the crop tight, y'see..."

He told me this in all seriousness, using his hands to demonstrate the stretching process, as though it were entirely plausible that I might one day wish to make a bull penis crop for myself.

Oh, yes, some of the Disneyland characters were most definitely colorful.

Our Three-Hour Tour

The reason tour guides came to exist in the first place, as the story was told to me during Tour Guide 101, is because a ticket seller from England named Cicely Rigdon caught the eye of a curious Walt Disney. He wondered why the lines at her ticket window were always the longest and slowest moving. Being the creative genius he was, he didn't simply tell her supervisor to advise that slow worker selling tickets to get with it. No, he watched and listened and ultimately interviewed Cicely to discover why the people stood in line for so long chatting with her. That didn't happen in any other line.

He found out that she tried to advise guests on a plan for getting the most out of their time at Disneyland. She would carefully plot out a route for them on the free guide book's map, noting the location of each attraction they hoped to visit. She told them about parades, entertainment, restaurants, and everything else they might want to know. She wasn't in a hurry to just scoot them through the line. She wanted to be sure the guests had the information they needed for a happy, successful day at the park before she let them go.

Walt Disney recognized a need that wasn't being met. A segment of visitors wanted to be personally taken in hand and shown how to best enjoy Disneyland. The concept of the ideal tour guide was Walt's own. It reflected his pride in the park and that he always wanted to be certain every guest who came had the best experience possible. Guides were meant to be the wholesome, girl-next-door type—even though two of the first five original tour guides were male. The most important part of this newly created job would be to connect with each guest on a one-on-one personal level, to make all of them feel welcome.

From those early observations, discussions, and interviews, the concept of the guided tour was born. The first tours went out in 1958, eleven years before I was hired. One of those original five guides was still working in the department then, but she wasn't leading tours. She was a "lead" and one of the nicest ever, although every lead girl was pretty special. There was a decade's worth of tour guide tradition established by 1969. It was a tightly run department with lots of inflexible rules, but despite that, we still thought it was the best possible job in the park.

British Cicely is now counted among the small group of elite Disneyland legends. She was tapped to head the new Guest Relations Department by Walt himself, and she helped to plan it all from the ground up. That's probably why we wore the Royal Stewart tartan, velvet riding caps, and carried English leather crops. When you see pictures of her back then, she had dark hair, sparkling eyes, and a gentle smile. By the time I met her, she was a honey blonde, those blue eyes snapped when she wasn't pleased, and the smile had grown somewhat more crocodilian. I may be one of the few guides who felt this way, or perhaps not, but since I'm the one telling this story, it's the only point of view I can share with you.

She was good at what she did, *very* good. When she ran Guest Relations, it was run well. She just wasn't someone I could ever particularly warm to. I never felt at ease in her presence. Maybe some of that stemmed from the first comment she made, after telling me to sit down, during my interview. "My, we're quite the person, aren't we?" All she had done at that point was briefly glance over my resume. Who *says* something like that to an eighteen-year-old kid looking for seasonal work? Who uses the royal "we"? Okay, who other than Queen Victoria?

Her snide comment highlights a schism that existed between the seasonal cast members and those who worked full time. When I was old enough to apply for employment at Disneyland, I had earned merit scholarships to college and won awards in areas as diverse as fine arts, community service, and academics. I participated in many school activities. A list of personal accomplishments was specifically requested by the Disneyland personnel office. The application asked us to describe achievements, academics, awards, and activities. I didn't walk in, sit down, and say, out of the blue, "Hey, let me tell you all about myself, and whoo, boy, I am *quite* the person!"

I discovered that Cicely herself experienced a bit of a sticky wicket getting a job in the park when she applied in 1957. She once recalled, "I made five attempts to get a job [at Disneyland]. The fifth time, I was finally hired, and I was so excited I came home and drove my car through the garage!"

A woman who needed to apply five times before being hired and who had been selling tickets at the main gate just a little over a decade before might well look at an application like mine and feel the need to take me down a peg, put me in my place, as it were. The three men who interviewed me before her could not have been any more pleasant or kinder, so her response was the anomaly that afternoon.

Most, if not all, of the part-time guides were in college and working to earn money for tuition. A few girls were financially well-off and were working just for the experience itself, but they didn't work any less hard than anyone else. They were from Newport Beach, Laguna, and other beach communities or the wealthy enclaves of Los Angeles. Their fathers were airline pilots, successful business executives, physicians. They took sailing lessons and went to Europe.

Maybe the pay wasn't fabulous, but it was certainly far better than other part-time alternatives. Compared with job opportunities that would be available to us in a few years, a full time guide would have just a fraction of that earning potential. If you weren't on the management track, and very few women besides Cicely were, it would be hard to support yourself. Many of the full-time girls rented apartments together. Disney has never been known for generously compensating its work force, except at the very top. The Native Americans who shared their cultural heritage, customs, arts, and dances in Frontierland since 1955 were summarily dispensed with in 1971, shortly after asking for more money. They swiftly discovered how quickly their ceremonial dance circle could be paved over to make way for Bear Country.

For the most part, the full-time tour guides were girls who had started to work right out of high school. My big sister Alexandrite was one of them. Many had been doing it for ten years. There was no requirement for completing any college coursework before the job could be done well. Practically every guide was under thirty years old. A lot of them had started work at the park in the late 1950s. Anyone, not just guides, who still held the same entry-level position ten or twelve years later was an object of compassion, not envy. Caste status in those kinds of positions peaked at about the age when most part-time employees would be finishing college. Age inversely correlated with status after that. If a person hadn't joined the ranks of management after ten years, it probably wasn't in the cards.

The full-time employees still in those entry level positions, more chillingly known as "lifers," knew each other well. They spent the long, slow, gray winter months together when they actually needed to wear those rain ponchos we only heard about. Their expectations and experiences were entirely different from those in the part-time crowd. If being a Disneyland tour guide was the highest professional goal a girl had, she didn't have a lot in common with a university student.

They were the girls Cicely Rigdon was particularly close to; the full-time girls and Cis spent a lot of time together and formed deep, lasting relationships. They felt genuine affection for her and she generously returned it. They cared about each other in a way those of us just passing though the Tour Garden never could. This doesn't mean that many part-time girls didn't also feel real affection for Cicely, but it was a different kind of friendship than the one she shared with the full-time cadre.

"I finally made it," Ruby told the girls gathered for a lunch break one day in the lounge. "I'm going to be a Pan Am stewardess!"

"When do you start?"

"The first of July!'

"Oh, that's really great!"

"Congratulations, Ruby!"

"I hope *I* get to be a stewardess someday," a full-time girl might wistfully add.

Ruby was so happy you couldn't help but appreciate her delight. She was looking forward to touring the world, maybe even meeting and marrying the man of her dreams. She was bilingual, beautiful, and would certainly be an asset to Pan American Airlines. Girls also left tour guide jobs to join the ranks of United or American. These were the days when you could fly round trip to San Francisco for $32. It was considered an exciting step up, and the pay was definitely better. The popular book *Coffee, Tea, or Me*, a fictional stewardess' "memoirs" ghost-written by a man in 1967, did a lot to glamorize and sexualize the profession in the general public's imagination. There was even a National Airlines ad campaign featuring stewardesses asking customers to, "Fly me!" That's right. "I'm Cheryl. Fly me! "I'm Jo. Fly me!" "I'm Laura. Fly me non-stop to Miami!"

My dad traveled often and was a frequent flyer before that term was coined. He was gone to San Francisco for one week out of every four and to Portland, Seattle, Butte, and Salt Lake City for two weeks twice a year. All the valets and ticket clerks at LAX knew him by name, as I discovered whenever I flew with him.

He usually took the airport shuttle from LAX back to the the Disneyland Hotel. On the way, he was surrounded by tourists heading for a vacation at the park. He loved hearing exchanges like this one, which happened frequently.

"Daddy, Daddy, is that Disneyland?"

"Yes, son, that's Disneyland." The child's father would nod in the affirmative with confidence.

Southern California is loaded with oil refineries and cracking plants, often located beside the freeways, which are used to break apart (or crack) molecules and form new molecules; the petrochemical plant is called a "cracker." It turns ethane into ethelyne. The plants are large, extensive structures with many tall towers. Everything is outlined in pretty little lights at night. Even if you don't know what the refineries are, they look attractive and intriguing. The airport shuttle bus breezed right by "Disneyland."

"Daddy, Daddy, we're passing it!"

A few minutes later, the child would cry out again, "Daddy, Daddy, is *that* Disneyland?"

"Yes, son, *that's* Disneyland."

It wasn't. There were several beautifully-illuminated cracking plants on the way to the Disneyland Hotel. Dad never tired of hearing this predictable exchange. Often, if our family were driving at night and passed one of the oil refineries, he'd chuckle to himself and say, "Look, there's Disneyland."

He enjoyed being something of rebel. When a stewardess would ask him, on one of his many flights, "Coffee, tea, or milk?" he sometimes mischievously chose another option.

Dad would cheerfully reply, "Pepsi, please!"

"Oh, Miss, I'll have a Pepsi, too."

"Me, too, Miss."

"Can I get a Pepsi?"

His order would touch off a deluge of demand for Pepsi up and down the aisles. It wasn't widely advertised, but it was available upon request in limited quantities. He flew a lot and thought the stewardess position was a "glorified waitress." It was demanding, difficult, and potentially dangerous. It was never a job I thought of as being desirable. I wouldn't have said "no" to the great travel benefits, and just because we didn't think highly of the job doesn't mean most people felt that way. Most girls, in fact, especially those not going to college, were captivated by the prospect of cute uniforms and high-flying romance that came with the position. Just as there were no tour guides much over thirty when I started to work, there were no aging stewardesses, either. Like a sparkler, that career was brilliant and over soon.

A guided tour was meant to last about two-and-a-half hours, but you could add an hour to that on very busy days. It included five attractions and one additional ticket good for anything else at Disneyland. In the Tour Garden just on your left past the left tunnel, you'd check in at the dispatch desk and meet your guide who would give you a triangular tag about three inches high. You could write your name on the tag and where you were from, but most people didn't. There was a little hole in the top through which a loop of string was tied. You would use the string to affix it to a button or purse so that it was visible. It would match the color of the one your tour guide had attached through the leather loop at the end of her riding crop. Tags were yellow, red, blue, green, and orange. Each tour that went out got a different color.

You'd then take your seat in the Tour Garden so you would be ready to begin your gay tour of the Magic Kingdom. That's just how the voice on the tape playing on loudspeakers at the main gate characterized it. Terminology changes. Very shortly after I started to work, the word "gay" was removed from the description of our guided tours.

"My name is Andrea, and I'll be your guide today."

I might ask you questions like, "Where are you from?" "How long will you be staying in southern California?" "Have you ever visited the park before?"

I liked hearing about all the different places the guests were from, and they were happy to tell me about them. Some, I had visited myself. I was always surprised at how very pale the legs were on people from colder climates. They'd be roasted lobster-red by the end of the day. Sunscreen was rarely applied. Nearly every guest I ever had on a tour was friendly and excited.

Guests, in turn, might ask me, "How long is the tour?" "What rides will we go on?" "Where's the nearest rest room?" There were restrooms close by just outside City Hall.

The moms and dads might want to know where I went to college. By 1971, I attended the University of San Francisco. Once they heard that, a lot of guys wanted to talk about the Dons' basketball team that had won the National Championship in 1949 and then again in both 1955 and 1956, thanks in large part to a young Bill Russell. It was still a strong program in the early 1970s when I was a student. Our hometowns, sports, current events, Disneyland history—there was always something of interest to chat about with guests. When about twenty people were waiting or ten or fifteen minutes had passed, we'd be off on our tour.

"Red tags? We're ready!" I'd call. "C'mon, folks, step right this way!"

Somewhere just outside the Tour Garden, guides would usually step up on a planter so that everyone could see and hear better. There was sometimes a scramble to claim a prime spot. I'd always ask guests to let me know if they couldn't hear me or if I were walking too fast or if someone needed to have something repeated. I always did my best to speak clearly and slowly, knowing that this was a lot of new information for them to absorb. I would always also tell guests to ask any questions they might have. In that way, it was a lot like teaching.

If you were a member of my tour, first, you'd hear a brief description about the opening day of Disneyland and a bit of background history. The story of those original orange groves, the plans and dreams of Walt Disney, and his words on the dedication plaque would be shared. I would tell you about the areas and lands we'd be visiting: Main Street, Adventureland, New Orleans Square, Bear Country (starting in 1972), Frontierland, Tomorrowland, and Fantasyland.

The first attraction was the Main Street Train Station. Our tour would board a steam train for a "grand circle tour" of Disneyland. You'd hear about Walt's long-time interest in trains and about his own little miniature railroad installed at the Holmby Hills estate. If we happened to be directed through the right side of the turnstile by a RETLAW conductor, we would pass by a display with Walt's original, lovingly detailed *Lilly Belle* engine, the one named after his wife, Lillian. Each of the authentic steam trains in operation had been refurbished after years of service, and they now circled Disneyland up to 13,500 times a year.

If you take a VIP tour today, you may be able to catch a ride on the pretty *Lilly Belle* car, decorated by Mrs. Disney with personal memorabilia from the family collection. It is the only one from Disneyland's opening day that is still running. The car is often only available at limited times and for limited groups, however, such as Club 33 members and special visitors.

As much as Walt Disney loved trains, I'd have thought the train ride itself might have been a bit more interesting. Mostly, what guests saw aboard the train was a series of tunnels interspersed with brief glimpses of the park, especially the undeveloped areas. The diesel fumes were strong. Every time I smell diesel, I'm transported right back to the Disneyland Railroad.

The first stop for guests boarding and departing was at Frontierland station. I would point out the beautiful New Orleans Square area and the "very spooky" Haunted Mansion with its "999 ghosts." A main benefit of the tour was to show guests things they would want to come back to and enjoy on their own later. It would have been nice to be able to take our guests on more attractions, but you could only do so much in what was intended to be a two-and-a-half hour tour. The length depended upon the number of visitors in the park on any given day. A day with 25,000 visitors expected was just about right.

We'd ride past the back of the Rivers of America and sometimes see the *Mark Twain* or the *Columbia* sailing grandly by. We'd view the back side of the Native American village, the burning cabin, the motionless deer, and the Native American on his pinto pony with his hand raised in greeting.

After I returned to work from college in June 1972, I was shocked to see an entirely new land had popped up like a mushroom in my absence just past the Haunted Mansion. As the train my tour was riding emerged from the tunnel, there it was! Getting back to the Main Street station once again, I parked my people for a minute and dashed over to the Tour Garden.

"Aqua, what's that land just past Frontierland?"

"Oh, yeah. It's new. It's called Bear Country, and you have to take your people over there to the Country Bear Jamboree. Can't miss it. It's at the very back of the area."

"Okay. Thanks!"

"...and *skip* the *Mark Twain*!"

"Got it!"

It was just that kind of bizarre experience that produced nightmares for me in the decades to come. I've never known anyone who has worked at the park who managed to escape having Disney nightmares. Mine often featured new lands inexplicably cropping up on a tour, completely unbeknownst to me. Other dreams were about lost shoes, shoes left behind in a locked car, having brought the wrong shoes to work. Those old Wardrobe bulletins about shoe requirements really played mind games. I dreamed of locker combinations forgotten seconds before I was due to lead a tour, of being on a ride that morphed into something entirely different like the time Small World became a submarine voyage through all the countries of the world.

For many years, I dreamed that I'd been called back to fill in because they needed more guides and didn't have time enough to train them. I'd see guides I didn't know, all of whom wore different costumes from those we had worn. I was supposed to lead a tour in German. The tour guide lounge had been moved. You name it, I dreamed it. Just as college students often dream they are in a strange classroom taking the final exam in a course they never signed up for and hadn't ever attended or actors dream they are on stage in a play but had memorized their lines from an entirely different play, if you worked at Disneyland, you'd be reliving it all through distorted dreams long after you had punched your last time card.

Until just a couple of years ago, I kept a couple of new pairs of red Pendleton wool socks in my drawer "just in case." It was like having tour guide post-traumatic stress disorder. Lots of the socks we checked out of Wardrobe were worn out and didn't have enough elastic to stay up. It was so annoying to have to stop and pull up socks every couple of minutes. You didn't want to get those, so I usually just bought my own. This all sounds uncomfortably like author James Clavell who had been interned in a Japanese concentration camp during World War II. For the rest of his life, he carried a little tin of sardines in his pocket because that was "enough to flavor a whole pot of rice." Just in case....

Still on the train, we would go through yet another tunnel and see the back side of Small World. Next stop was the Tomorrowland station where I'd point out the PeopleMover we'd take later. That wasn't a very cool ride, but it provided an overview of Tomorrowland and all that it had to offer, much of it at no charge. I'd then deliver the information about the best tunnel of all, the one filled with dinosaurs shipped back to us from the 1964–1965 New York World's Fair. This was, by far, the best thing about the train ride.

First, we'd hear the gentle music of an orchestra playing "The Grand Canyon Suite" and see that natural wonder unfolding behind glass, depicted as it looks today. Wildlife like coyotes, rabbits, pumas, bighorn sheep, wild turkeys, quail, and bald eagles were displayed in their realistically created habitats.

The tunnel would darken, the music would become menacing, and our train would slowly pass by the Grand Canyon as it might have looked in primordial times when "dinosaurs roamed the earth." These were the same dinosaurs we were expected to warn our guests not to feed, according to our spiel. I'd say that to kids sometimes or maybe on a Spanish tour. The Latino population was always ready to share a good laugh with me. They were so much fun.

First was the relatively benign scene of the plant eaters, brontosaurus families up to their bellies in water, giant insects, pterodactyls, triceratops eggs hatching with Mama beaming proudly—this was bucolic in comparison with the final display where a tyrannosaur is fighting to the death with a stegosaur. Red lava erupts from an angry volcano. The cornered little guy swings his spiked tale bravely at his attacker. You just know it's going to end badly for him. The T-Rex's little rubbery arms shake in rage; his open maw is lined with rows of teeth like knives. His jaws snap as he lunges. Close your eyes, kids. Nobody's thinking of feeding this guy!

Back on Main Street again, we'd head down the ramp and pause once more. I would share some statistics (like the park is about 70 acres and the parking lot 100). I loved telling guests about this turn-of-the-century area, a "typical small town that could be found anywhere in America about 1890–1900." The Town Square, Bank of America, Mr. Lincoln, Main Street Cinema (one of the few things I never visited myself), Flower Mart, General Store, and the Emporium were all pointed out as we passed by them. This was the point at which I was supposed to share the "paid all the hay they can eat" joke about the draft horses pulling the street cars. Don't hold your breath waiting for it.

At the Central Plaza we'd stop again. From there, it's very easy for guests to see that the lands really do fan out "like spokes on a wheel." I'd use my trusty crop to point out the original four lands, each visible from the plaza. Central Plaza is also, I advised, a good place to meet if anyone in your party becomes separated. No lost children's names would be announced over the loudspeakers. They'd be kept at City Hall until they could be reunited with their families. There were no cell phones, either, so it was always a good idea to decide on an easy place to meet.

As we entered Adventureland, I would point out the Enchanted Tiki Room, talk a bit about audio-animatronics (*audio-animatrónicos en español*), and mention the gorgeous Tahitian Terrace restaurant for a "Polynesian meal in an island atmosphere." Tours used to take the Jungle Cruise, and I wish we had, too. It's such a fun attraction. The only time we could ride it was when something else was "down." This is where the "crocodiles are very fond of red"—or green or blue or whatever color tag my group was wearing—joke would be delivered.

Passing the Jungle Cruise, I'd tell my people to be sure to come back after the tour. Walt loved it best, and it's easy to understand why. We'd step out of the main thoroughfare of foot traffic near the Swiss Family Robinson Tree House. If you haven't seen the 1960 film, or haven't seen it in a while, do. It's hilarious, fabulous, vintage Disney. The top level was eighty feet above the ground and provided a great, panoramic view of the entire area. This was all set atop the infamous banyan tree, species *Disneydendron*, covered with "300,000 hand-painted blossoms and leaves." We told our people that some of the original sets and props from the movie were used throughout the three levels of the treehouse. That thrifty recycling of movie props was something Disney was always *very* fond of doing.

We went on Pirates in New Orleans Square, a highlight of the tour. It was the best attraction in the park, always popular. New Orleans was added when the Rivers of America underwent an expansion in the mid-1960s. It was a perfect addition. The queues could be long and winding at Pirates, especially during those hot summer months. A forty-five minute wait wasn't uncommon. After pointing out the Blue Bayou as we floated by, we'd enjoy the cool, dark ride filled with life-like pirates, life-like blazes, the skeleton crew, and mountains of fabulous treasure. I never met anyone who didn't love this attraction. Following the boat's long, jerky climb back up the ramp, we'd disembark, head out into the bright sunlight, and take a ten-minute break.

Rest rooms, restaurants, and wonderful shops meant the break was over in the blink of an eye. Once, I was unable to locate a family on my tour. That happened so rarely. Finally, after waiting as long as we could, we followed one of the winding streets out of New Orleans. As we passed the French Market Café with its expansive outdoor dining area, there they were just digging into a full spaghetti lunch. They looked at us, surprised. I tapped my watch to indicate time was up, and then some.

"We'll look for you on our way back from Bear County," I told them.

Before 1972, the next attraction on the tour was the *Mark Twain*. (After 1972, it was the Country Bear Jamboree.) The *Mark* wasn't an exciting attraction, but it was certainly gorgeous. The boat looked like a three-tiered wedding cake with its intricate, white, lacy balustrades. The cruise around Tom Sawyer Island was leisurely. You'd see "river traffic" like that found on the rivers a hundred years ago. We saw the Mike Fink Keel Boats, the log rafts that would later ferry Yippies to the island, and the Indian War Canoes. We were supposed to call Tom Sawyer Island "Parent's Paradise" because the kids could play in the cave, Fort Wilderness, and on a suspension barrel bridge, without getting lost. I called it Tom Sawyer Island.

If the park were particularly busy, the Sailing Ship *Columbia* would be backed out of its dock to join the *Mark* on the Rivers of America. It was "a full-rigged, exact replica of the first American ship to sail around the world." The *Columbia* had just one deck, was painted bright orange, and had no private lounge with couches, all distinct drawbacks.

Starting in summer 1972, we headed through Bear Country to the theatre at the back where a band of singing bears would serenade us, country-style. Country music was highly popular at that time and was definitely mainstream. It was a long way from the days of Tex Ritter, Hank Williams, and Bob Wills. There were two identical theaters running the same show. The most we had to wait was about twenty minutes.

The bears were very cute. One was called Liver Lips, the band was the Five Bear Rugs, Big Al was an enormous cowboy bear, Trixie was a tearful bear unlucky in love, and the master of ceremonies had a raccoon cap on his head that turned out to be an actual raccoon who joined in the fun. Three little girl bears in sun bonnets sang about not getting the guy they wanted, a song that was later borrowed for a skit for the tour guide banquet.

Every time I meet a guy that gets me shook,
All I ever get from him's a dirty look,
It's the same way everywhere I've found,
All the guys that turn me on turn me down.

Beautiful "Swinging'" Teddi Barra came down from a hole in the ceiling, reminiscent of the descending cockatoo girls in the Tiki Room. She swings back and forth over the audience wearing a feathered boa and big, floppy hat.

Looking back it seems a bit silly, but we all clapped for the audio-animatronic bears just as if they had been real performers. We did that twice a day. The show was adorable and was popular with our guests, regardless of which language they spoke. The tunes were catchy and a lot of fun.

After watching the Country Bears, we'd cross Frontierland and head back for the hub. On the way, I would point out the gold-and-white theatre that housed the Golden Horseshoe Revue, which always had a big crowd waiting. The original show played from 1955 until 1986, more than 39,000 performances. There is a good reason the show ran so long: It was outstanding. Regardless of what Disneyland replaced it with, if I had my way, I'd recast the show with new faces and stage it exactly as it was written. It could run another thirty-one years! At the University of Disneyland, we were told of one older couple who came *every* Sunday to see the show. Eventually, they were awarded free lifetime passes to the park, back when when year-long admission passes to Disneyland weren't available to the public. Still in Frontierland, I would also point out the Mine Train Through Nature's Wonderland and the "other Frontierland train, the four-footed Pack Mule Train."

Next, it was back through the log entrance to Frontierland and over to Central Plaza. Expansions were planned to keep each new attraction within a short walk of this "central point." My guests were a lot more familiar with the park now. They'd been to Main Street, Adventureland, New Orleans Square, Bear Country, and were ready for the final two lands.

Here, we guides told our guests that over half-a-million flowers, shrubs, and trees were planted annually, vegetation that was imported from all parts of the world. There is a perfect view of the drawbridge to picturesque Sleeping Beauty Castle, a drawbridge only lowered twice in park history: on the day Disneyland opened to allow children to rush into Fantasyland, and again in 1993 for the opening of New Fantasyland.

Heading through Tomorrowland from the plaza, we'd make a beeline for the PeopleMover. It ran on elevated tracks overhead, four orange cars in each section coupled together. Each car held about four people. Sometimes, you might see a tour go by with the guide sitting alone in the last car. That didn't happen often, but when it happened to me, I'd kick off my shoes and put my red-stockinged feet up on the seat opposite mine for a few minutes of down-time before the tour's conclusion. We told our guests that the

PeopleMover "may be a prototype of conveyances in the cities of tomorrow's world." Well, if our PeopleMover was any indication, the number of serious accidents might outweigh any potential benefits. At two miles an hour, it was slow, but it was also the site of many accidents, some of them serious.

Every once in a great while, just as we left the PeopleMover and I had finished telling a group about the planter that was actually a bandstand at Coke's Tomorrowland Terrace Restaurant, it would suddenly rise up out of the ground as if on cue with a live band playing some catchy rock tune.

"How'd you *do* that," some impressed guest would always ask.

I wish I knew. If I did, I'd pull that rabbit out of my hat for every tour.

As we passed the Submarine Voyage attraction, we'd stop to look into the crystal-clear blue waters of the lagoon filled with colorful sea life. Just as having live animals on the Jungle Cruise had been initially proposed, there had been some talk about putting actual sea creatures in the lagoon. Cooler heads prevailed, and all of the sea creatures were replicas. I'd always direct my people back to Submarine Voyage once the tour ended with Small World. It was close enough for them to easily find and was a fantastic adventure.

Although the passenger seats on the subs were under the water level, the captain's orders to dive or climb were met only by a rush of tiny bubbles past the portholes. Through those portholes you'd see mermaids—not the living ones of yore—swimming in circles with long hair flowing behind them, sunken ships, an undersea volcanic earthquake, the Lost Continent of Atlantis, and a cross-eyed sea serpent that caused the pilot to become incredulous. "Great Scott, you're right! It's a sea serpent!" he says to the first mate.

Opposite the subs was the always-formidable line of people waiting as long as a couple of hours to ride the Matterhorn bobsleds. We'd point out the 146-foot-tall mountain, a replica of the famous Swiss peak. It felt like those bobsleds were going a lot faster than 27 miles an hour! There were two separate tracks with ten cars running on each. The ride lasted over about two-and-a-half minutes. Most of our guests were not the kind to ride the Matterhorn, but if they did decide to brave it, we'd warn them about getting wet at the end. The bobsled splashed down into the stream pretty hard and you'd get sprayed, especially if you were sitting in the front seat.

We passed Autopia where Ron once got a pretty serious whiplash after he had come to a stop at the ride's end. A kid behind him deliberately rear-ended his sports car going full speed. The monorail station was in Tomorrowland and so was one of the two Skyway stations. There were Rocket Jets, the Journey Through Inner Space, and the Flight to the Moon.

Finally, our tour was drawing to a close. We'd pass by Storybook Land and see the little boats of guests being swallowed by Monstro. Walt Disney, like a lot of people, had a fascination for miniatures. So did Walter Knott over at Knott's Berry Farm. There were perfect little plantings and intricately detailed scenes from children's stories brought to Lilliputian life. Toad Hall, Cinderella's Castle on a hill, the houses of the Three Little Pigs, and Pinocchio's Village were depicted. My favorite part was the living patchwork quilt, different tiny plants and succulents in every square stitched together by ropes that resembled thread. The Casey Jr. Railroad ran alongside. We'd briefly mention all the rides in Fantasyland, but again, most of our tour groups wouldn't be candidates for the wildly spinning teacups on Mad Tea Party, Dumbo, Alice in Wonderland, Peter Pan, Snow White, or King Arthur Carrousel. Fantasyland was filled with kids and almost always busy.

It's a Small World, "the happiest cruise that ever sailed," was our final attraction. Some of the trees in the topiary garden had been started in 1960 and were fascinating, especially for those of us who had never seen that kind of thing before. The voyage through the lands of the world was always received with kudos from the guests. It took me awhile to warm up to it, but once I did, I loved seeing the delighted reactions of the guests, especially those from other countries who saw the dolls of children from their respective homelands singing in their own language.

Once the boats brought us back and the tour had finished, we said our good-byes next to the topiary garden. I reminded the guests about the attractions they might want to visit, places to eat, and any special entertainment available that day. This was our scripted good-bye:

> I want to thank you for giving me the opportunity to tell you about the hopes and dreams that have made Disneyland a reality. Walt Disney often said that Disneyland would never be completed. From our original 22 attractions on opening day, we've grown to more than 50 today, and we're planning even more new things for the near future.

By 1971, we were supposed to give a pretty extensive sales pitch for visiting Walt Disney World in Florida at the end of our tour. People, at least those I met, did not want to stand in the hot sun after completing a three-hour tour and listen to a litany of the "four miles of beaches," the "43 square miles" of land, or the fact that "we think of Walt Disney World as the 'Vacation Kingdom of the World,' a destination resort where your family can spend an entire vacation." Yes, I might mention it in passing, but my guests were here to see Disneyland, the park Walt himself created, not to hear a page-long breathless description of the glory that is Walt Disney World. They were ready for lunch, and so was I.

I always said a warm and friendly good-bye to the people on my tour, but it was genuine and unscripted, and I certainly wasn't acting as a shill for WDW. Then, it would be a quick walk around the Matterhorn, past the Central Plaza, down the right side of Main Street, and back to the tour guide lounge. After a quick lunch, it was time to do it all over again with a new group of guests. In the immortal words of Herman's Hermits, "Second verse, same as the first...."

Anything Your Heart Desires ... on a VIP Tour

For years, VIP tours were led only by VIP hostesses. Every one of the hostesses I knew had started in Disneyland as a tour guide, and most of them were permanent, full-time employees. Some were married. A couple of them had small children. They were a little older than the guides, could speak more foreign languages, and had a special aura. When one of them walked into the lounge, conversations among the rest of us often stopped because they might have something funny to say or juicy to share about a tour they had just finished. We looked up to them and respected their greater wisdom and experience. Just as I was hired, however, it was decided that the tour guide and the VIP hostess positions would be combined. All of us had to be able to lead both kinds of tours, which was an exciting prospect.

The costumes they wore were meant to seem more like regular outfits, not so much a costume but a dressed-up look. The first time I worked at the park over Christmas break in 1969, the VIP girls wore dove gray wool skirts, pale pink satin blouses, and burgundy-colored velvet jackets. Ever since, I always think of that combination as the very height of fashion. They never wore hats, but they still wore the big, gold "D" pin and their name tag like us.

It was generally from this VIP group that future Disneyland Ambassadors would be chosen, although occasionally it was a tour guide instead. VIP hostesses were in an exalted category all their own, and I never met one who wasn't as kind, friendly, and sweet as she could be. The same, unfortunately, couldn't be said of every tour guide. The VIP hostesses were genuinely great at what they did and didn't lord it over the rest of us. It wasn't the easiest thing for a neophyte to walk into a group of girls so tightly knit as this one, but they were welcoming and helpful to us from day one, and it was something I always appreciated.

In summer, their costumes were more casual. The look switched to a red, white, and blue ensemble, red vest with blue piping over blue skirt with long-sleeved white blouse. Then, it was a sleeveless, "mod" orange dress with white piping, pretty swingin' for the times. Nothing, for me, though, ever quite measured up to that gray, pink, and burgundy VIP hostess costume of my first Christmas, maybe because none of the girls in my December orientation group were experienced enough to lead a VIP tour yet, so I never got the chance to wear it.

If you had the money to book a VIP tour, you could set your own agenda. It was very expensive when compared with any other way to see the park. Today, the cost for a VIP host or hostess runs between $400–550 per hour, and you are required to reserve your VIP host or hostess for at least six hours. That price doesn't include admission he the park, either. You need to pay for that, too. You do get priority seating for the parades or special entertainment, a benefit not on offer when I worked at Disneyland. In the early 1970s, guests paid handsomely for the individual attention from a private hostess, but the price was nowhere near as expensive as it is now. The shortest VIP tour I ever led lasted about four hours. The longest one lasted all day. No more than ten guests can accompany each host or hostess nowadays, but I once led a VIP tour with twenty businessmen from Mexico.

Our VIP guests also paid for anything they or their hostess ate or drank. The hostess had to remember all of the attractions her party visited because they had to all be listed and tallied up for billing once the tour was finished. VIP guests were charged for riding each one of those, too, although they were *not* charged for their hostess to ride. A VIP tour did not allow anyone to cut the line unless there were some political or physical reason for doing so.

Nikita Kruschev, then the Premier of the Soviet Union, was famously refused a tour of Disneyland in September 1959 because it was deemed too much of a security concern to guarantee his safety. He was highly upset at the time and said so. The translation of his remarks upon hearing the disappointing news illustrates his frustration:

> And I say, I would very much like to go and see Disneyland. But then, we cannot guarantee your security, they say. Then what must I do? Commit suicide? What is it? Is there an epidemic of cholera there or something? Or have gangsters taken hold of the place that can destroy me?

Well, it's understandable. Who wouldn't be upset to find out he couldn't go to Disneyland?

It was the task of the hostess to find out what her party wanted to do, make suggestions if she thought the guests would enjoy something they might not have heard about, and to be agreeable, entertaining, and informed.

Anyone who was famous or infamous had kids or grandkids who wanted to come to Disneyland, just like everyone else. When they came, they would usually pre-order a VIP tour. It was always so exciting to hear the VIP hostesses share a few details of what the tour *and* the celebrity been like. There was no set plan to follow, so every VIP tour was different. You gave people exactly what they wanted, anything their heart desired, and some of them desired plenty. The VIP hostesses never gossiped, at least not to us, but they sometimes let slip a few fun details, enough to make us long for the day when we, too, would be leading a celebrity around the park.

Disney stars like Burl Ives took a VIP tour. I crossed paths with Burl in Club 33. So did film stars like Yul Brynner, who was dressed all in black, smoking one cigarette after another, and much shorter than expected, and Sammy Davis, Jr., walking jauntily up Main Street with his beautiful wife, Altovise. Every time I was out on a regular tour and noticed a VIP hostess walk by, I'd try to see who might be trailing in her wake. Sometimes, with the sunglasses, it was hard to tell.

Even in the years before she was Murphy Brown, actress Candice Bergen was immensely popular, and her parents came for a VIP tour one summer. Her dad was the hugely successful ventriloquist Edgar Bergen who, along with his sidekick "dummies" Charlie McCarthy and Mortimer Snerd, was famous on the radio, in films, and on television. At the end of the tour, Bergen told VIP hostess Amethyst that she reminded him very much of his daughter. She was walking on air to be compared to Candice Bergen by Candice's own father! He and his wife both garnered rave reviews from their hostess. Just imagine the biggest stars of television and film, sports stars, politicians, well-known musicians, all spending an afternoon with you! It sounded almost too good to be true. I couldn't wait. Unfortunately, like many things in life, at least sometimes it *was* too good to be true.

I spent the vast majority of my time leading regular park tours, two a day. Every once in a while, however, each one of the tour guides was given a VIP tour to lead. What follows is a description of the three main types of VIP Tours I led during my three summers working at Disneyland.

Let's Get Down to Business

I had been given my VIP assignment the night before, so I had already checked out the red, white, and blue costume from Wardrobe and put it on in place of my tour guide uniform. Instead of hanging around the tour guide lounge or garden waiting for a tour or going out to meet the buses, I walked over to the Guest Relations booth just through the tunnel past the Bank of America on Main Street. Opal, an experienced tour guide, usually worked the booth. She was extremely good at it, too.

My heart sunk a little as I faced some twenty somber men in dark suits, not a movie star or celebrity in the bunch. My heart sunk a little further as it dawned on me that they were conversing amongst each other in Spanish. By this time, my four years of high school language classes had been supplemented with a year of college Spanish and lots of Spanish tours, so it wasn't completely daunting, but it meant I wasn't going to be able to relax much and would have to concentrate on things like the pluperfect, subjunctive, and preterite imperfect verb tenses, and work hard to recall my sometimes ludicrous-sounding translations of Disneyland jargon. *Los submarinos*, for example. As if it would take five years of language study to get that one. Oh, and what should I call Winnie the Pooh? Certainly *Winnie la mierda* wouldn't sound at all appropriate!

Before I could worry about it any further, Opal beckoned me over happily. Sure, she was happy—she didn't have to lead this gloomy looking bunch around the park for six hours.

"Señor Rojo, I'd like you to meet your VIP hostess for today. Andrea, meet Señor Rojo. He and some of his colleagues will be your guests today." She grinned. I managed a tentative smile.

"*Buenos días, Señor. Un placer de conocerle.*" A pleasure to meet you. And then to the group (that's *grupo* in Spanish), "*Encantada, señores.*" Enchanted sounds a bit much in English, but it's just fine in Spanish.

At that, the serious businessmen broke into wide smiles and began instantly nodding their heads excitedly, waving their hands, and speaking Spanish a million miles a minute ... and all of this at once. Anyone who has studied a foreign language knows that's one of the biggest problems to overcome when conversing with a native speaker. Your teacher speaks slowly and clearly, but real people don't. No, real people slur their words, use slang, and generally don't take a breath. Oh, this was going to be a loooong six hours.

One thing you learn very quickly about leading tours in Spanish, however, is that *todo el mundo hispánico* (everyone in the Hispanic world) is as excited and happy as can be that you took the time and effort to learn, and even sometimes to butcher, their native tongue.

Señor Rojo was smiling the broadest and nodding the most emphatically of them all. He was a nice-looking man of middle years, graying a bit at the temples, impeccably groomed, and extremely gracious and eager to show his guests a nice day in the park. Well, so was I. This wasn't going to be too bad, in spite of my earlier concerns. In fact, it actually turned out to be lots of fun for all of us. This tour might look all business, but the guys were definitely here for a day at Disneyland, just like anyone else. If you think, as I did at first, that the VIP tours were just for celebrities, you'd be wrong. A lot of them were exactly like this one, for company executives who wanted to entertain their business colleagues.

Señor Rojo was *el presidente*, the president, of a major Mexican national airline. He was charming, gregarious, and very anxious to enjoy himself along with his entourage. I wanted to show him and his guests most of the E-ticket rides that day, although we would probably skip the Matterhorn if I had anything to say about it. Mexico City where he lived had the biggest roller-coaster in the world at that time in Chapultepec Park. I had just been there with on a high school foreign language field trip in 1968, the year of the Summer Olympics in Mexico. Riding it had been a lot like I imagine it would be looking over the railing of the Empire State Building and jumping. I have never experienced anything like that before and hope to never have that dubious pleasure again, not unless someone holds a gun to my head and insists.

So, we'd follow the usual "grand circle tour" of the park on the train, stroll down picturesque Main Street, U.S.A., and visit Adventureland next. That's still the way I like to do the park. The Jungle Cruise is always a sure-fire crowd-pleaser, and this was definitely a happy crowd ready for some big fun.

I dusted off my old reliable Jungle joke and delivered it in all seriousness: "*Que tengan mucho cuidado, señores, porque los cocodrilos les gustan*—insert color of tag here..." (It means roughly, "Take great care, gentlemen, because the crocodiles like—") Uh-oh. I usually just insert the color of whatever triangular tag my *grupo* happened to be wearing that day, but none of this bunch wore a tag. No one on the VIP Tours did.

I suppose I could have said *rojo*, which means red, but that seemed less than tactful, considering Señor Rojo was my guest's name. I didn't want to insinuate that the crocodiles would probably eat him. Quickly, I inserted *gris*, which mean gray, because most of them happened to be wearing dark gray suits. The color joke always got a big, appreciative laugh, and this time was no exception. They pointed at each other's gray suits and chuckled. Some made snapping noises.

Har-har-har. They continued to laugh as we boarded the boat for our journey through the jungle. Some twenty hands were raised politely to help me aboard. This was an extremely gallant *grupo*, for sure. Hispanic men always were. No translations needed to enjoy this trip, but the skipper's awesome jokes and puns didn't get a laugh like my corny one did, merely because no one could understand what he was saying. The wild animals and characters tell their own story, though, and the attraction is plenty interesting enough on its own.

In rapid succession, we visited Pirates, Haunted Mansion, and the *Mark Twain*. I took *el presidente de la compañía* up into the wheelhouse on the *Mark* so he could "steer" her around Tom Sawyer Island, and he enjoyed it like a kid. You're never too important or too grown-up for Disneyland, or at least that's what I always believed—until the next tour I'll describe, that is. Señor Rojo earned his riverboat pilot's license and was beaming as we rejoined the rest of the men, somewhat envious that they had not also earned pilot licenses. Next up, lunch at Club 33!

It was elegant and special, as always. El señor and I took the lift with the attendant while the rest of the gang walked up the stairway. There was a room full of animal-head trophies and horns mounted on the walls as we passed though. If you've ever seen Jim Carey in *When Nature Calls*, you'll be able to easily picture it—minus the screaming. A long table was set for our party in the main part of the dining room near the ornate old harpsichord sitting in a corner in gilded splendor. Everything was tastefully decorated, from the framed prints on the wall to the snowy linens and silverware on our table, and, back when smoking was far more common and less restricted than it is now, black souvenir matchbooks embossed with "Señor Rojo" and "Club 33" were set at every place. El presidente presided at the head of the table with me on his right to translate.

You order whatever you like at Club 33, VIP hostesses as well, and this experience most definitely wasn't old hat for me by any means. I tried the lobster crepes which were delicious. A lavish, sumptuous buffet was arrayed artfully on a long table near the harpsichord. Everything that was served looked just as fantastic, and the group from Mexico had a rollicking good time over lunch. They drank, I didn't, and then I signed for our lunch because nothing as crass as cash ever visibly changed hands on a VIP tour. It was all oh-so-discreet. No worries, however. He'd most assuredly get the bill as he left the park that afternoon once the tour was finished.

Later, in the tour guide lounge, I told some of the girls about the amazing lobster crepes I'd had for lunch. Amber, the always-opinionated guide from France, shuddered. "Isn't that fattening?" she sniffed. She had married an American guy and was having issues adjusting to life in the USA.

"Definitely."

I was not about to order a lettuce leaf with dressing on the side at Club 33, however. I rarely got to try something that fancy.

Amber did, however, teach us how to pronounce crepes correctly, something I've always remembered. We used to say "krāpes," rhymed with grapes, but now I pronounce it "crrreh-ps," with the crrreh part gargled in the back of the throat. Don't even get her started on the way we Americans mangle the word croissant! She even had to have a special phonetic name tag made because no one pronounced AHMBEHR right, either.

"Señorita Andrea, I'd like to offer you a round-trip ticket to Mexico City on my airline to thank you for this fantastic tour," Señor Rojo told me graciously as our delightful lunch was drawing to a close.

Now, if you know anything at all about the wonderful, generous people of Mexico, you know they will routinely offer you anything and everything including the shirt off their own backs. "Oh, you like my pen? It's yours—keep it." They even have a saying: *mi casa es su casa*, my house is your house; *los méxicanos* are the most hospitable people I've ever met. That's why they were nearly universally a joy to have on tour. Okay, just once I did have a grumpy older Spanish gentleman who kept correcting my every little *verbo* tense slip, and I realize there were plenty, but that only stands out because it was so completely unusual.

We were not allowed to accept tips, so I thanked him profusely but firmly turned down his kind offer. He was completely serious, and I'm quite sure he would have gladly followed through, but that is much too much for what amounted to taking an immensely likable, polite group of men from Mexico around the park, lunching at Club 33, and having a great time.

The remainder of our tour was spent taking a relaxing tour of Tomorrowland on the PeopleMover to let that luxurious lunch settle, and we caught the easy-going submarines (*los submarinos*) after that.

"Oh, that?" Hard to miss the mountain. "That's the Matterhorn bobsled attraction, but it's not nearly as spectacular as yours in Chapultepec, Señor." Whew. Dodged that one.

Back then, Fantasyland had one E-ticket ride, Small World, or in this case *el mundo pequeño*, and it was always the perfect end to a tour, particularly one packed with visitors from a different country. *Bienvenidos* (welcome) sign at the beginning, *adíos* (good-bye) sign at the end, and a whole bunch of busily dancing, smiling *muñecas* (dolls) singing in Spanish without once losing their collective breath, gamely represented all regions of Mexico. There is even a volcano just like Popocatépetl firing off in the background.

If you haven't seen an entire boatload of sober-suited businessmen simultaneously levitate off their seats with delight, you just haven't lived. My all-time favorite part is when guests point out something cool as if this is all new to me, too.

I just smile, nod, and maybe say something like, "Oh, how adorable," while thinking "You know, I must have missed that on my first *FIVE HUNDRED TRIPS*."

In all seriousness, though, that is part of the fun, the charm of leading a tour. You actually *do* see everything there with new eyes when you take a group through what is, to a tour guide or VIP hostess, an extremely familiar attraction, especially a group as clearly delighted and amazed by what they see as this one.

The next tour I'll tell you about was extremely low on the charm or joy meter by comparison, and it was VIP tours like it that made me happy with my usual assignment leading regular tours, the ones where the vast majority of my guests were easy to please and were simply joining a tour to have a good time at Disneyland.

Oh, Sing Sweet Nightingale

The night before, I had been told I would have a celebrity VIP tour the following day. Exciting! Lead Girl Garnet usually knew who it would be, and she told me. I recognized her name right away, of course. Everyone did back then. She was a famous folk singer and a fantastic, successful songwriter, immensely popular. I really liked her music and looked forward to the tour. The afternoon was bright and warm, sunny as usual in the southern California summer months. There was no meal scheduled to work around. No reservations had been booked, which was kind of unusual. Most VIP tours did book a lunch or dinner. This one was scheduled to last just four hours, and when I heard that, I was a little disappointed. My disappointment at the abbreviated length of the tour didn't last long.

That day, I wore the orange-and-white hostess dress. Groovy. Again, I went to the Guest Relations booth to meet up with my guests, four people including the famous singer. This time, however, there was no wide, welcoming smile from Opal. She was basically unflappable and had seen it all, but that afternoon she looked concerned and motioned me through the little door to the booth where she sat perched on a stool.

"There's a problem. Her date can't get in dressed like that. His hair's too long, but they're going to let that slide. Not the clothes, though. He's wearing stuff that's ripped with lots of holes in the shirt. Definitely too scruffy for Disneyland!" she told me with a worried frown.

After the Yippie invasion in 1970, security hosts were enforcing far stricter dress-code regulations for guests than they had before that date. Rules like these hadn't been adhered to for many years, but after August 6, 1970, things abruptly changed. The dress code hammer came down.

I peeked out through the Guest Relations booth window and immediately saw the folk singer. Along with just about everyone else in America, I recognized that stunning visage from any number of album and magazine covers. Her high cheekbones, long, straight hair with bangs, and wide-set blue eyes were so familiar. She was truly gorgeous, exceptionally striking, but she didn't look happy, not at all. This tour was getting off to an inauspicious start. Then I saw her date corralled behind a chain fence in a sort of holding pen. He looked no happier than she did. Next, there stood the singer's agent and his very young date. He looked the least happy of them all. The girl with him merely looked bored. I don't think I heard her say two words the entire afternoon, although she did laugh at any remarks the agent made.

It was determined that the singer's date, a singer himself but not nearly as well-known as she was, could enter the park if he bought and wore some kind of acceptable T-shirt available at the nearby souvenir stand. By the time this was accomplished, it was difficult for me to believe that I was anywhere near the Happiest Place on Earth.

He shrugged the shirt on unhappily, and we four were introduced by Opal. The singer, at least, smiled briefly, and she had a thousand-watt smile. It didn't reach her eyes, though. I had no idea at the time of the currents and undercurrents of tumultuous emotions running through this little group's inter-personal dynamic. When people seem unhappy, it's usually because they are. Later, I would learn some of the reasons why, but for now, I only knew something was definitely off. Then, we were all off—on their tour.

For the most part, guests gladly interact with their guides. They look to us as their lifeline in navigating the unfamiliar rapids of the park. We are there to help them have a great time. Why *wouldn't* they want to establish some kind of friendly rapport with the person who was going to be hanging out with them for the next several hours? Not these four, however; they spoke only to each other, *sotto voce*. Their low, confidential tones made it impossible for me to hear anything. I was being deliberately shut out and could feel my face flaming by the time we hit the middle of Main Street. As guides, we knew pretty well how to reach out to nearly everyone on some basic level. There's usually *something* of interest to chat about. Not this time.

Finally, we hit the hub where the four lands fan out "like spokes on a wheel." I stopped and turned around to face them. After all, they'd need me to get them on the attractions, and I still had no idea where they wanted to go or what they wanted to see.

"Tell me a little bit about what you'd like to see and do this afternoon," I said. I tried to smile, but it felt more like I was gritting my teeth. No smiles back, of course.

Four pair of half-closed eyes evaded mine. Maybe there were a few side whispers to each other, but there was nothing said to me. It began to get even more uncomfortable.

At last, they seemed to reach some kind of telepathic consensus.

"Let's go on Dumbo!" the agent suggested to the others. He tried to sound both enthusiastic and sarcastic at the same time, which is a neat trick if you can manage it. "Oh, and let's see Mickey Mouse!" he threw in for good measure.

Then it dawned on me. They were here to ridicule Disneyland, not to enjoy it. Things went downhill from there, and they hadn't exactly started out on high ground as it was.

The agent had recently scored an enormous financial deal, and along with it, he had made a fortune, but that was only a tiny fraction of his vast net worth today. Now, he's one of the biggest entertainment moguls on the planet. In 1972, he seemed decades older than me, but he wasn't. He was actually very young. He was from a large city on the other coast, and some of the people from there were quite different from us Westerners, the tour guides discovered. They could be blunter, although they'd call it honest. They could be ruder, although they'd say they were just "telling it like it is." Most of all, they could be very difficult to please.

That's why, when tour guides heard that a big tour from this particular agent's home town had shown up at the Tour Garden, there was a frantic, mad dash and thunderous scramble out the back door. This guy might have been exceedingly rich, and he was, but he was exceedingly poor in the basic human values we learned, shared, and believed in at Disneyland.

It was the longest four hours I have ever spent in the Magic Kingdom. They wanted to do and see anything that could be considered campy, anything corny. Dumbo, Peter Pan, the 1968 Academy Award-winning animated short film *Winnie-the-Pooh and the Blustery Day*, Snow White—I wondered if we would ever get out of Fantasyland. They wanted to eat at the Carousel Corner. Just regular folks yuckin' it up with the masses. I'd be willing to bet that the Carousel Corner didn't see many VIP tours from the surprised look on their faces when I signed for the order. This group was not interested in any E-ticket attractions. Quite the reverse. Everywhere we went, they laughed, and these were not nice laughs, either, but snide ones. The famous singer seemed a little embarrassed, but maybe that was just wishful thinking on my part. I loved her music, so how could she laugh at my park?

Eventually, we ended up at the GE Carousel of Progress. I had never viewed it ironically. I thought it a charming look at how electricity made people's lives easier and more pleasant. It started with Dad, Mom, Sis, and Bro with funny Grandpa appearing in guest spots that consisted of slice-of-life, typical family events. Here was Grandpa sweltering in a bathtub of water wearing a striped men's bathing costume in front of a block of ice with electric fan pointed at it. No air-conditioning back then, by jingo. There was Mom, cooking a Christmas dinner in just minutes in the near future. Well, hey, that actually happened. It was the advent of the microwave. There was also a shaggy pooch for added warmth and humor.

That had to be the absolute nadir of the tour. No matter what the audio-animatronic family did, my cool quartet ridiculed them. They snorted and sniggered like naughty kids. The agent was definitely the ring leader, but while some class clowns can be innocuous, even good-natured, others are definitely mean-spirited. Every comment was pointed, every jibe hurtful. He had hired me to take them around my beloved Disneyland so he and his group could laugh at it. I was never so glad to see the end of a tour as I was that one! Never.

As the GE family cheerfully sang, "There's a great big beautiful tomorrow, shining at the end of every day," we exited down the long ramp. Without ever really meeting my eyes or saying much of a good-bye, they must have been as relieved to be on their own as I was to be rid of them. Now, they could feel free to make fun of everything to their heart's content and as loudly as they liked. The unhappy little group took off one way and I took off the other. It was a relief to be heading back to the time shack. I was shell-shocked. I had earned my money that afternoon and just couldn't wait to get back to my regular routine the next day.

Celebrity tours? If this one were any indication, I'll pass.

A Dream Is a Wish Your Heart Makes

The last category of VIP tour I'll discuss is the one I could have gladly led all day, every day. These were the tours that warmed your heart and made you glad you worked at the Happiest Place on Earth. Sometimes, very ill children are granted a wish by a philanthropic organization, a once-in-a-lifetime visit, a dream come true, and sometimes, that wish is a trip to Disneyland. Consider yourself fortunate if you get to be a part of making that happen.

One of those tours I remember in particular was with Tommy and his charming family. Tommy was a frail little guy, shorter and slighter than average for his age, which was about ten. His mom and dad and big sister could not have been any nicer or more excited. They appreciated everything we did. They loved it all. The family was making memories to last a lifetime, and from what I understood, Tommy's lifetime wasn't going to be as long as most people's. He had, he explained to me without a hint of self pity, cystic fibrosis. I'd never heard of it before.

"It's not exactly fun," he said, "but I get used to it. They have to cup their hands," he continued, pointing to his parents who sat there listening with smiles. How they managed that was incredibly moving, a testament to the way Tommy himself was able to cope so well. "Then, they have to hit me really hard going up and down my back until I can cough up a bunch of stuff. They need to do it a couple of times a day." Their smiles never cracked.

It was an education to me. Throughout the course of the day, I continued to hear more about the illness and came to understand it better. Later, my son went to school with a friend who had the same disease. Her family had moved to Iowa City because of advances being made in the treatment of cystic fibrosis here at the University of Iowa Hospitals and Clinics, and I only hoped that some of those advances had come in time to benefit Tommy as well.

We had been on all of the E-ticket amusements we could possibly squeeze into one jam-packed day. By the time we got to Frontierland, it was time to take a break. We sat in a private box in the old-time Western dance hall, the same box Walt Disney himself had always used, right up on the stage.

We had yummy snacks while enjoying the good old Golden Horseshoe Revue, longest running show in the history of show biz. It's still a Guinness Book world-record holder.

Nobody laughed louder than Tommy when Wally Boag spit his "teeth" all over the theatre after being slapped in the mouth. No one whistled any louder for raucous Slue Foot Sue, played by the beautiful Betty Taylor, as she teased the men in the audience with her mirror and feathered boa. She even blew Tommy a little kiss. People in the boxes often get special treatment, and I could have personally kissed Sue myself for making his day so special. No one cheered the pretty can-can girls dancing on the stage any more vigorously. Fulton Burley, the Irish tenor, had eyebrows he could make dance almost as vigorously as the girls could high-kick. He'd always been a favorite of mine, ever since he told me I had a face as sweet as Shirley Temple's. Fulton was an old-school entertainer, and the show was reliably uproarious.

Tommy loved everything we did all day long, and so did his family. They were incredibly grateful. It was as if everything had been personally created just for their enjoyment. They treated me like I was a member of their family, too, even if just for the day. I've noticed that people most times reciprocate how they are treated, and I just couldn't do enough for this wonderful family. It felt a lot like taking my own out-of-town relatives to the park.

Finally, the day was drawing to an end. The family and I sat next to the water in the lovely Blue Bayou Restaurant watching the quiet little boats full of people go by in Pirates while waiting for our dinner. Monte Cristos all around, please! The ambience there is authentic old New Orleans. Fireflies seem to flit among the cattails, a rocker rocks on the dilapidated porch of a wooden fishing shack. From inside, a banjo twangs softly. In the distance, once a boat drifted by, we would hear a high-pitched collective scream in the distance.

"What's that?" Tommy asked, not at all apprehensively. This spunky kid was game for anything. "How come they're screaming?"

"Oh, you'll see. Just wait. After we eat, I'll let you find out for yourself." That's the way my cousin Matt had introduced the ride to us, and it's really the best way. Dinner in the Bayou, then go see what the screaming is all about.

By this time, Tommy fairly wiggled with excitement. His eyes shone and danced in the glow of the candlelight just like the fireflies. From a corner, the talented trio of jazz musicians who came to us from New Orleans every summer played their set. Is Disneyland really magical? At that moment, I felt the magic touch us all very softly, and that feeling is with me still. For children, it is always very close to the surface. J.M. Barrie knew that when he penned *Peter Pan*, but it's really still there for all of us. You just need to give it a chance—be ready for it when it comes.

Date Nite at Disneyland

Spending all day making sure everyone *else* has a wonderful time visiting Disneyland can, and often does, lead to an incredible amount of pent-up demand to have some of that fun yourself. One perk that went a long way toward alleviating the demand was a fondly remembered summer tradition known as Date Nite.

All day long in the sizzling summer sun, we wore elaborate, hot costumes. Not Mickey Mouse or Donald Duck hot, but still very hot. Appropriate wear for a southern California July is *not* wool knee socks, long sleeves under a vest, a tie around your neck, a "skirt" that was actually designed to be modest culottes with a panel of extra fabric between your thighs, and a velvet hat on your head trapping in every last degree of heat. No, that's most assuredly not what any sane person would choose to wear for a day at the park when the weather forecast called for one hundred degrees or higher.

One sweltering afternoon in 1970, when I felt I would go stark raving mad if I didn't take something off, I actually threw caution to the wind and removed my strapless bra during the second tour. Okay, not in view of the guests because I'm not insane, but still it was quite the daring choice. After Pirates, we'd always take a ten to fifteen minute break in New Orleans Square, a perfect spot to stop.

While my tour group slugged down their alcohol-free mint juleps and munched on those heavenly, fragrant beignets, I slipped into a rest room stall, slipped out of the offending article, and slipped it under my riding cap. Most of the guides affixed long barrettes, one on each side of the cap's bill, to keep it from falling off. I'd never lost a cap before, but I crossed my fingers and toes just for insurance. There was a lot riding on keeping that cap in place that afternoon, namely my job. For me, practically always a good little rule follower, stashing an undergarment beneath my cap was tantamount to an open act of rebellion.

That day, I felt like Popeye wearing a kilt: That's all I can stands, I can't stands no more!

Relieved to be returning without incident to the tour guide lounge after the afternoon tour was finally finished, I stepped into the cool interior of the room that was packed with exhausted guides in varying states of undress. Socks were rolled into balls on the floor, vests scattered across the couches, caps sitting on the counter in front of the mirrors.

"Thank you, everyone, and I hope you all have a wonderful day here at the Magic Kingdom," I announced, taking a deep bow with a flourish and nodding my head vigorously so that my cap flew off. Along with it flew my bra.

First, disbelief. Then, stunned silence. Then, giggles.

"Are you *serious*?"

"When did you do *that*, Andrea, on Small World?"

"Oh, my gosh, I don't *believe* it!"

Well, I didn't quite believe it myself, but it sure felt good. Liberating, even. It was an act of defiance never again repeated, by me at any rate, but it was also an incident recalled wistfully that summer when the weather was so hot I could hardly stand it. Thankfully, this performance was not mentioned to Cicely or a supervisor. At least I don't think it was.

Requirements for the cast members were both strict and strictly enforced. We stood while our guests sat. We were never, under any circumstances, allowed to drink or eat anything when a guest might observe us. We couldn't use the rest rooms or lean against anything for support. While I could understand the intent behind those rigid rules, I'd be willing to lay odds that the people who created them never had to lead two tours a day during the summer months dressed, as we guides were, for the Happy Valley Hunt Club. We couldn't even stop at a water fountain to take a quick sip, something that in retrospect sounds like a recipe for heat stroke or worse.

Despite these daily draconian demands, one of the nicest benefits that came with a job at Disneyland was Date Nite. Most of us seasonal cast members were college students, and every penny was pinched. If I saved practically all of my summer paychecks, which I did, I was just able to pay for college expenses when those paychecks were combined with a couple of academic merit scholarships I had earned. To get in free meant $7.00 saved, and that added up.

Now, the 1969 $3.50 price of admission seems like such a fantastic bargain, especially when viewed in light of the current price of Disneyland admission, edging very close to $100. In today's dollars that $3.50 would be more than $23, and with inflation at more than 500% in the years between 1969 and 2015, the nearly $100 cost of admission today today would have been $14 back in 1969. That *still* would have been prohibitive for most families.

In 1969, you could get a whole ticket book for just $5.75, and for that price you also got admission to the park and to fifteen attractions. In today's dollars, the cost would be about $38, which is a lot less than the nearly $100 charged today! I always felt that you got your money's worth back then. Compared with other options, Disney was a good value. It remains a good value, but no matter how you slice it, the relative cost of going to the park has risen a lot faster than inflation.

The guided tour was $6.50, which included six rides, and some of the best ones. For first-time visitors, it was a nice option. Not only that, you were "taken on an exciting tour of Disneyland by a charming (*ahem*) guide who tells the fascinating story of the Magic Kingdom's history and growth." Don't forget, this was before a million-and-a-half guidebooks were written clueing people into all the ins and outs of getting the most from their visit. Even so, being led from one land to the other with a "charming" guide pointing out things to come back to later on was reassuring for people who had never before seen Disneyland except on television.

The general admission perk all the cast members received on Friday nights didn't include riding on anything, but there was so much to do that it really didn't matter. There was always something going on at night, so much so that they even had an official marketing name for it—Disneyland After Dark. Every cast member was allowed to bring in one guest on any summer Friday night, starting at 6:00 p.m. and staying until closing time. Couples lined up at the Guest Relations window to the right of the main gate, the same one where the VIP tours were met. You showed your employee ID card and you and your date were admitted, as simple as that.

Walt Disney visited every amusement park he could when planning the Magic Kingdom; most of them were great at providing examples of exactly what *not* to do, but one gave him inspiration. Tivoli Gardens in Copenhagen, opened in 1843, was clean, beautifully landscaped and impeccably maintained. It was lit at night by hundreds of thousands of tiny, white lights. It lent an aura of magic to the Denmark park, and it was something Walt replicated at Disneyland.

Twilight comes relatively early in Anaheim, California, with its southern latitude. Sometimes, it starts getting dark about 7:30 p.m. If you happen to be at Disneyland then, you'll see everything change. Each tree is lit with beautiful lights that twinkle among the leaves silhouetted against the dark blue night sky. The berm carefully shuts out the glow of neon that results from the surrounding suburban sprawl spilling over from Harbor Boulevard, Katella Avenue, South Walnut Street, and Ball Road.

The lights outlining all the buildings on Main Street come on at once, and the effect is dazzling. It's like seeing a Christmas tree light up every single night. You can smell the perfume of night-blooming jasmine, the sweet smell of hundreds of roses, the sharp scent of banks of petunias. Even if there were nothing else going on, just being in the park was enough.

Bands of all kinds played nightly. The Disney Marching Band pounded out rousing Sousa tunes and stirring, patriotic marches. They'd intersperse those with the music of familiar Disney animated feature films. The Kids of the Kingdom performed their little color-coordinated hearts out, squeaky clean and wholesome. Rock music played in Tomorrowland, although nothing more radical than "Jeremiah was a bullfrog...." The friendly trio in New Orleans Square played soft, lively jazz tunes that hung suspended on the warm night air. You might hear ragtime from the honky-tonk piano player over on Main Street or see the barbershop quartet ride by singing "Daisy, Daisy" on their famous bicycle-built-for-four. There were spectacular parades, an impressive nightly fireworks display, and entertainment of all kinds, which meant that you could always find something exciting to do. With operators who had seen you come through their turnstiles twice a day, you were often just waved on through with no need to produce a ticket.

It was so much fun to show my boyfriend, Ron, everything that I'd been telling him about all week. One thing he never grew tired of was touring the park with someone who knew the ropes. We didn't miss a Friday night. What else was more fun than Disneyland?

"Wait, we can't just cut in front of all those people, can we?" he asked, the first time I breezed through an empty lane with not a soul in sight as the jam-packed line of people next to it glared daggers at our rapidly advancing backs.

"No, this is okay. Both lines are open. It's just that everyone always gets in the one on the right. They think the left one must be the exit, but that's always in another place entirely," I told him. "We're fine, honey, c'mon!"

Soon, you'd see people ducking under or clambering over the ropes to fall in right behind us. Shortly afterwards, however, it would go back again to just the right line being full and the left one deserted.

Whenever you go to the park, *always* check to see that both entrance lines are being used. If it's not roped off, that means it's open. Feel free to walk right in. No kidding. Many times you'll pass a half-hour long waiting line and be able to board the attraction in no time at all. No matter how many times we did this, Ron always felt like we were pulling a fast one. Don't get me wrong. He loved it, but he always felt that this must be some kind of closely guarded secret only the *cognoscenti* were privy to. He was right, of course, but that's what made it such a guilty pleasure. If a cast member is standing there at the entrance, she'll say, "Use both lines, please," using the classic, inoffensive, Disney two-finger point, but if not, you can *still* use both lines and save yourself a ton of wait time. Just be sure to remove those daggers from your back before sitting down on the ride.

For me, one of the best parts of the evening was, in fact, just sitting, Coke in hand, watching the passing parade of people. That was my guilty pleasure. We couldn't sit or drink during the day while on stage, so you can be sure I'd do plenty of both on Date Nite.

One night, we heard a man calling to his wife who had walked on ahead with the kids.

"Hey, Shrimp!" he called.

No response. We chuckled. Perhaps that was a term of endearment between them, something along the lines of *chiquita* (not the banana kind) in Spanish or *ma petite* in French. After all, weren't all couples as head-over-heels in love as we were?

"Hey, Shrimp!" he called out again, louder this time.

Still no response.

"Hey, *FAT* SHRIMP!"

Okay, maybe there was nothing endearing about it after all.

Now *that* got her attention. Her expression as she wheeled around to face him might have made Ursula herself think twice about tangling with this particular corpulent crustacean.

Ever since, we'd use that memorable expression when trying to get each other's attention, and every time it absolutely cracked us up.

I'm not sure about the other cast members on Date Nite, but one thing I couldn't wait to do was poke my head into every shop on Main Street that I'd passed by during the week. There were so many, and we had to sail right by every one of them four times a day, going out on tour and coming back—twice.

The Hills Bros. Coffee House smelled heavenly first thing in the morning as I crossed Main Street heading for the tour guide lounge. It was not as appealing after 6:00 p.m., however. There was always the Emporium for the coolest souvenirs and best selection, but that could wait until we were on the way out. I loved the pretty jewelry store and still have a very sweet little ring Ron got for me there one Christmas. The Crystal Palace was dazzling in its array of gorgeous, sparkling treasures, none of which we could even think about purchasing. We could look, though, at no charge. After all, where would we even put an elaborate blown-glass galleon? Or a unicorn? A fantasy castle?

We had our silhouettes done at the popular Silhouette Studio, and the artist did a fantastic job in just a couple of minutes. It was uncanny, and all done freehand. Years later, we would add silhouettes of our two children. The price was reasonable and the quality exceptional. We'd pass by the Flower Mart filled to overflowing with baskets and carts of artificial flowers, not nearly as gorgeous as the real thing growing in every available pot or inch of soil wherever you looked.

I've always been a big Hallmark fan. Walt Disney lived for a number of years in Kansas City, Hallmark Company headquarters, and there was a large, prominent Hallmark store on a corner of our idealized version of Main Street, U.S.A., making it easy to find just the perfect card or gift.

"Do you mind if I take a quick detour through Hallmark?" an attractive young lady asked me when my morning tour group departed from the train station and set off down the right side of the street as tours always did, heading north towards Sleeping Beauty castle.

"No problem. I love it, too! Go right ahead. We'll just be walking down the street until we get to the hub, so you can meet up with us there," I advised her. "I'll watch for you, but if you miss us, we'll be heading through Adventureland toward Pirates of the Caribbean."

"Great. Thanks!"

As she rejoined us, I noticed she carried a little bag from the store.

"They always have super things, don't they," I asked, nodding toward her recent purchase.

"Well, I think so," she smiled, "but then I'm probably biased. My last name is Hall. It's my family's company." She didn't say it grandly, and she wasn't on a VIP tour. She was proud that her family had a store in this wonderful setting, and she had a good time seeing it for herself, as well she might. I have rarely met anyone on a tour as nice as she was, as sweet and appreciative, and as absolutely modest. Not only that, I was pretty relieved that everything I'd said about Hallmark was positive and enthusiastic. Walt Disney, it turns out, was a personal friend of the Hall family.

There was an old-time market on the far end of the street on the east corner with comestible treats from days gone by. Huge dill pickles swam in brine, cracker barrels were placed casually around the wooden floor, and a wide selection of jams, jellies, and other goodies were on plentiful display. You really could imagine yourself back in 1900 as you shopped. There was even a barber shop, a fully-functioning Bank of America, and a tobacco shop (yikes) complete with a wooden Indian (double yikes) on the street in front of it. The tobacco shop was in business from 1955 to 1991. By 1999, no cigarettes were sold in the park at all. By 2000, smoking was restricted to just three areas.

One of the most popular shops was the Candy Palace, and for good reason. The smells emanating from it were enticing, intoxicating even. You could practically feel your body levitating, wafting through the door on the heady scent of chocolate like Goofy, floating a couple of feet above the ground with your nostrils flaring in and out. It wasn't just the smell, either. You could actually watch the ladies making the sweet treats for sale. Buttery English toffee rolled in chocolate and crushed almonds, enormous lollipops made of tightly rolled concentric circles of molten sugar in every color of the rainbow and a few not found in nature, thick, gooey fudge—how could you choose? Nothing was too expensive, and you could buy the items in whatever amount you wanted, so we could usually find something small to take with us as we left at the end of the evening.

One thing I bought immediately after being hired was a big Mickey Mouse watch with a wide red band. Most cast members wore them. I loved it. Ingersoll made some of the early ones. The store on Main Street was a Timex shop. It was a perfect watch, reasonably priced, and something I kept for years. And true to the Timex advertisements of the day, it "takes a licking and keeps on ticking." One day I left it in my unlocked car in a parking lot at the mall and it was gone, but I still have the Cinderella watch with its now-faded blue fabric band that came in a glass (plastic) slipper that I got when I had my tonsils removed. The slipper is long gone.

Walking hand in hand, Ron and I could linger, take our time window shopping, maybe buy a trinket or two and generally do anything and everything that was strictly forbidden to me during the work day. He was ridiculously patient and let me fulfill every little whim I'd harbored all week long. Frozen banana? Okay. One of those New Orleans beignets? Why not? If you've never had one, what are you waiting for? Imagine a pillowy soft, square puff of deep-fried dough dusted with powdered sugar, warm and melting on your tongue. Tiana had it right in *The Princess and the Frog*. Those things are positively lethal!

We could even stop at every single drinking fountain we passed if we wanted to, not that we did. I'm not sure if anyone else indulged themselves nearly as much as I did, or as gleefully, but those special Friday nights were some of the best times we ever had, times we looked back on fondly in the decades to come. The twinkling lights in the park, a canopy of stars overhead, and the opportunity to sit, to eat, to drink, to lean, to buy—sheer bliss!

Once in a great while, we would have a real celebration and treat ourselves to an actual sit-down dinner at the Bayou or the Tahitian Terrace, a tropical paradise of a restaurant in Adventureland next to the Jungle Cruise that was located just past the iconic Enchanted Tiki Room "where de birds sing words and de flowers croon...." It was outdoors, lit by Tiki torches at a time when Hawaii had been a state for just over a decade, and everyone was enamored of flowing muumuus and flowered leis. Yes, it was Tahitian, not Hawaiian, but back then no one was bothered by such fine distinctions.

"Let's sit in the back," I told Ron as we entered the rattan-rich environment of the restaurant. It was embraced on all sides by lush bamboo and a forest of palms.

"Why? Can't we see the show better from down front?" he asked. "There are still plenty of open tables."

"Sure we can, especially if you'd like to be *in* the show, honey."

Ron was as shy as I was, even though he had played lead guitar in a rock band in high school and through most of college. He could do that in the same way I could pretend to be an extrovert tour guide. Once you were on stage, you got into character and it was fine.

"What do you mean?"

"Would you like to dance the hula up there with the girls?" I asked him innocently. "If you would, then by all means, let's sit down front." We had been dating exclusively for about nine months by this time, and I knew very well what his reaction would be.

"Oh, my gosh! No! I would so *not* want to dance the hula in front of the whole restaurant," he said, rapidly grabbing me by the hand and making a beeline for the raised dining platform located at the very back of the restaurant.

From then on, that's where we always sat, and in the last row if at all possible. I had seen the hula dancers twining their arms persuasively around male diners and dragging them onto the stage to dance with them. Some guys, you know the kind, just love that kind of wild thing and really get into the hip-shakin' spirit of the islands. Others, like Ron, would have been positively mortified and couldn't wait to slink back to their seats when their public humiliation at last came to a red-faced end.

Still, until the grab-and-dance part of the show was over, Ron never could truly relax and enjoy his coconut-crusted shrimp and pineapple rice. He'd look everywhere but at the girls trolling the captive audience for partners. Once that bit was done, he'd breath a gusty sigh of relief, smile, and thoroughly enjoy the rest of the show. Guys danced with flames, girls demonstrated how to tell a story with their graceful hands, and the food was always spectacular, but dining at the Terrace also carried with it just that hint of the potential for a humiliating hula experience, something that made the Bayou a safer choice.

Since our tours went on the same five rides *ad infinitum*, it was nice to check out what the rest of the park had to offer. The Jungle Cruise was always fun, and since most of the skippers knew us guides, we often came in for a bit of good-natured ribbing.

"Oh, look, folks, we have a pair of love birds with us in the boat this evening—those two can (get it, *toucan*) sure bill and coo!" one might observe, or the ever-popular cast shout-out when one cast member recognizes another, "I smell pixie dust...." or just, "Oh, so *now* the tour guide decides to grace us with her presence."

The Haunted Mansion had opened in August 1969 to great fanfare, so it was still new, highly interesting, and very rarely a part of our tour. It isn't really scary, but it's probably best to avoid with younger children who might be with a tour group.

Once while I was area hostessing in New Orleans, a guest asked me, "Where's the Ghost Shack?"

Knott's Berry Farm, a smaller theme park with an Old West-style vibe, was located just down the Santa Ana Freeway in Buena Park, and it *did* have something called a Haunted Shack.

"The Haunted *Mansion*," I corrected gently, pointing with my trusty riding crop, "is just down this street and to the left."

Ghost Shack? How déclassé. We were awfully proud of our elaborate, gorgeous ante-bellum mansion, which could not be considered a "shack" in any sense.

Since we never took the tours to Fantasyland, except to Small World through the "back door" from Tomorrowland, we had fun on those Friday nights going on cute Mr. Toad or Peter Pan or Alice, just because Ron had never ridden any of them before.

He hadn't grown up with the Disney movies as I had, either. I felt like his Disney literacy just wasn't up to par, so in the days before VHS or DVD, we always tried to catch one of the classics at a theater when they were showing. Eventually, he saw them all and, I'm happy to say, came to adore them as much as I did. He even teared up when it seemed loyal bloodhound Trusty wouldn't survive his run-in with the wagon in *Lady and the Tramp*.

Fantasyland attractions weren't crowded in the evenings after the kids had gone home and to bed. Believe it or not, there were actually times back then when the park wasn't crowded at all. Today, you need a game plan with all the spontaneity of the D-Day invasion of Normandy to visit the park, but when I worked there, it was still entirely possible to visit everything you wanted to with absolutely no sign of a minute-by-minute itinerary, FastPass, or magnetic wrist band. By the way, those Walt Disney World MagicBands are a game-changer. Come on, Disneyland, get with the times.

We enjoyed visiting the One of a Kind antiques shop in New Orleans Square and the sweet-smelling Mlle. Antoinette's Parfumerie where they would mix a custom scent just for you. I had to be careful about explaining that particular offering on tours because sometimes ladies would walk into the shop and expect the poor guy behind the counter to whip up a concoction based on what he thought would match madame's personality. Uh, not quite. You pick and choose the scents you like, those are combined, and the formula is noted in case you wish to order it again. They don't take one look at you and design a perfume based on your perceived likes and dislikes!

Lafitte's Silver Shop, Cristal d'Orleans where the immensely talented Arribas brothers got their start, Le Gourmet with its high-end kitchen gadgets, Café Orleans with those juleps and beignets, and the cafeteria-style French Market Café all made New Orleans Square one of the nicest little corners of the park to hang out.

When we got tired toward the end of the evening, we could ride one of the steam trains around the perimeter for a while or hop on Tomorrowland's two-miles-per-hour PeopleMover, no longer in operation. Since those were both on the usual tour, I almost always knew the operators and we could ride free. Fireworks over the Matterhorn capped off the evening, and then it was time for a leisurely stroll back down Main Street and out the front gate.

"Wait, let's stop of the Candy Kitchen! Oh, and I want to get that darling photo frame I saw in the window at the Emporium." We didn't usually get out of the park without something to take with us.

I always had Sundays and Mondays off, the two days with the lightest attendance, so after Date Nite, I'd be up the next morning and heading to Anaheim for a busy Saturday at Disneyland. My shift usually started about 9:00 a.m. No matter how many times we went, and we went often, Date Nite never got old.

If the point was to familiarize the cast members with all parts of the park, that was certainly accomplished. I could speak knowledgeably about all kinds of things that weren't on our tour and could recommend shops where just about any kind of gift or souvenir could be found. You want a restaurant recommendation? I've got lots. Casual? Sit-down? Want me to describe the benefits of a frozen banana? Date Nite was the surest way to be sure we all knew the park inside and out. By the time our daughter worked at Disneyland, it had sadly become a thing of the past.

That's too bad, because Date Nite at Disneyland really was the nicest possible way I can imagine for a cast member to spend a summer Friday night.

Muy Pequeño el Mundo Es —Very Small the World Is

As you can see by this chapter title, literal translations don't always manage to completely capture the spirit of the original, in this case "it's a small world after all." We tour guides did our best to accurately translate Disneyland for our guests from all corners of the globe. Sometimes, that was easier said than done.

The inspirational message of hope, peace, and happiness is lovingly brought to life by the dancing, singing dolls representing children from many of the world's cultures on It's a Small World. Twice a day, we guides listened to that message with our little boatloads filled with intrepid guests. It was always the last stop of the tour and one that enveloped everyone in a cozy blanket of warm, fuzzy feelings. People of all ages and nations usually adore this attraction and leave humming its catchy tune, smiles on their faces mirroring those worn by the multicultural brigade of mannequins inside the elaborately decorated, golden-and-white filagreed clock tower.

Let me confess before proceeding any further with this chapter that I was one of those exceedingly few curmudgeonly individuals who was not immediately captivated by the charm of this much-loved attraction. It opened at Disneyland in 1966 following its debut at the 1964–1965 New York World's Fair. Enormous fanfare and hoopla accompanied the grand opening. I'm not sure about the rest of the nation, but we in southern California were treated to extensive coverage of the event.

Children "from many lands" dressed in traditional folk costumes gathered at the entrance. A bottle filled with "waters from around the world" was ceremoniously emptied into the highly chlorinated canal. Walt was there, basking in the goodwill engendered by this new attraction. It had been sponsored by Pepsi at the fair and, by the time I took tours through it, by Bank of America, a natural choice because of the long-time partnership existing between the bank and Disneyland.

I went to see Small World for the first time in 1966 during a parent-teacher conference day off from high school with three friends. We were excited to finally be able to see this wonder for ourselves. Three out of four of us were enchanted, as promised. One wasn't. I can vividly remember my sharp disappointment looking at the vignettes of many lands and thinking, just like the plaintive inquiry in Peggy Lee's famous song, "Is that all there is?" The dolls were cute. Their ethnic costumes were, too, and the song itself quickly became one of the most recognized ear-worms in the world. There was no way to find fault with the optimistic message.

What I took issue with was the simplistic construction of the scenes themselves. You could see "the little man behind the curtain" all too clearly. The glitter looked like glitter, not stardust. The cellophane rain in the tropical rainforest looked like exactly what it was. The fan-activated fabric in fiery shades of red and orange blowing from the volcano's erupting peak was quite clearly fabric and not lava. When you looked over the edge of the canal, all the poles and boxes and supports were visible. Yes, they were painted black, but that didn't make them disappear. The ceiling looked uncomfortably like those drop-down panels in our classrooms at school. Was it too light inside? Was that the issue?

If it had been darker, maybe the seams and bolts might have disappeared, the imperfections faded into the background as they did on the dark rides in Fantasyland. As we rode though this highly-anticipated attraction, all I kept thinking was, "Other than the dolls, my dad and I could have made this stuff in the garage with some sheets of plywood and a jigsaw." Not the animated figures but the sets seemed so simple, and not in a charming "childlike" way. All I felt was duped. It was too easy to see reality lurking just beneath the tapping toes of all those darling dancers. My friends got out of the boat gasping in wonder at how amazing it had all been. They had exactly the kind of response you were supposed to have. Not until hundreds of times later floating past those same simple scenes with the guests of my tours did I catch a glimpse of the magic for myself, and then it was magic reflected in their eyes.

It meant so much for people who had come from different parts of the globe to see their homeland depicted, their culture, and to hear the familiar tune sung in their own language. It's hard to describe the electricity that ran like a current through the boat as soon as the first of my guests from Mexico saw the marketplace, the folk dancers dressed in the lacy, white style of Veracrúz, those *caballeros* and *señoritas* dancing around the iconic sombrero in their "hat dance" and belting out "...*muy pequeño el mundo es.*" As you realize now, the sentence literally means "very small the world is" as opposed to "it's a small world after all." Everything loses something in translation.

For years, on many hundreds of trips through Small World, I thought the muñuecas from Mexico were singing *"un pequeño el mundo es,"* which would mean "a 'little one' the world is." Fact-checking recently, I was shocked to find out they had been singing *muy*, not *un*, all along. The "jolly-fried-eggs" and "bugs on the saddle" phenomena of misunderstood song lyrics had struck again!

An electric spark of recognition at seeing their homeland leaped from seat to seat, from person to person. They might get a big charge out of the adorable little laughing hyena and the kids from Africa giggling along with him or the Australian mama kangaroo rocking on long feet with a joey snoozing in her pouch, but to see their own heritage recognized and celebrated positively captivated them. To say they were enchanted is no understatement.

Seeing that emotional, visceral response again and again, and not just from those on my Spanish tours but from guests representing a myriad of world cultures, it would have been a very curmudgeonly tour guide indeed who could fail to be deeply moved. Through the eyes of my guests, I, too, came to love It's a Small World. I've never entirely managed to see past the seams and joints so visible to me in 1966, but I have learned to ignore them and focus instead on the message and the magic of it.

Dealing with thousands of people from all over the United States and from countries around the world was one of the best educations a college student could hope to receive, and it was not one that could ever be gained from a book or in a classroom. We didn't just meet and greet people, either. We spent hours socializing with them, chatting, listening, sharing ideas and good times with each other. They wanted to know all about California, my home, and Disneyland, my park, while I wanted to hear as much as I could about wherever they might be from. Two-and-a-half or three hours seemed hardly enough time, but day after day, month after month, Disneyland's tour guides came to appreciate different points of view in a way few people will ever have the chance to do.

"Two busloads of Aussies due here in fifteen," dispatcher Aquamarine called loudly into the lounge where several of us sat waiting for our shift to start.

"Count me in!"

"Me, too!"

"Dibs on one of those tours!"

"Hey, you guys had the Aussies last week," Diamond wailed woefully—and futilely—from a restroom stall, but no one was listening. By that time, three of us, the three lucky enough to be ready to go and not in the rest room at the time the clarion call came, were already dashing out the door and heading for the bus parking area.

That's the way it always went when Australians came to Disneyland. I don't know what made them so much fun, but if the ones we saw were in any way representative, that is one seriously rockin' country. The Aussies were funny, exuberant, easy to please, and just plain nice.

"Good arvo, 'ow yar goin', mates? No drama. Unless you're knackered, let's be off 'cause this park's ripper." Their slang is as adorable as they are!

California translation: "Good afternoon. How are you doing, friends? No problems. Unless you're too tired, let's get going because this park is really great!"

It was always a scramble to claim one of the buses full of friendly Australians. You could most assuredly count on several delightful hours in their company. They loved everything we did. They laughed at anything even remotely funny that we said. They made working at the park a sheer delight.

The New Zealanders and the Tasmanians were cut from the same golden cloth as the Aussies. Those groups were in equally high demand by the guides. They would come with tiny pins from their countries and share them with anyone and everyone lucky enough to cross their path. Small, perfect kiwi bird pins, a tiny map of Tasmania, a clever kangaroo—we collected them and wore them with pride. Those folks from "down under" had practically everyone else on earth beat in terms of charm. When we climbed the stairs to board one of the buses, we were greeted by an overwhelming roar of applause, hoots, whistles, and cheers. We could never get enough. Wouldn't it be great if everyone were like that?

Unfortunately, they weren't.

One big city in particular became known for producing some of the most difficult guests we ever had to deal with. They were from our own country, but as far as we were concerned, they might as well have been from another planet. If you hadn't traveled much and leading a tour was your only exposure to people hailing from this city, you might be excused for thinking that you'd be just as happy staying right here in California for the rest of your life.

This is just one minor incident, but it sums up for me why people from there were among our most unpopular guests. In three years, I had never had a complaint expressed either to me directly or to my supervisor about a tour I led. This event happened in 1972, my last summer working at Disneyland. By that time, I was a very experienced guide and thought I'd seen it all. Turns out I hadn't.

We began, as usual, with a train trip around the park. I loved it when the special steam locomotive lovingly restored and refurbished from its years working on a Louisiana sugar plantation pulled up. Its seating was actually more authentic than those that had been refitted with two long banks of park-facing seats. That afternoon, sure enough, the old plantation steamie pulled into the Disneyland station. We took the trip around the perimeter and all twenty-some guests and I disembarked from the train.

"Wait! We want to complain to your boss!" one of the men shouted loudly. Initially, I thought he must be joking. Other than the train ride and a brief introduction to Disneyland's history, nothing had happened. We had visited pleasantly enough in the garden shortly before the tour started.

"About what? Is there anything I can do to help?" At first, I honestly figured he was clowning around like some guys do, just trying to be funny.

When I saw the angry expressions on the faces of the two couples, however, I quickly realized he meant business.

"We paid good money for a tour and you didn't tell us that we should have sat on the outside seats. That's where all the stuff that we were supposed to look at was, and we couldn't see." He was jabbing his index finger angrily toward me. "Show me where to complain."

Good money? I didn't realize there was any other kind.

"The train has a lot of short rows of seats. There is no way to put every person on a tour on the outside and have other people at every stop climb over you." People getting off the train right now, in fact, were trying to get past him, but he didn't budge. "That's not how they load the train. I have no control over it. The conductor loads the cars," I attempted to explain.

Meanwhile, the other sixteen guests with me were staring uncomfortably at the ground, the sky, anywhere but at us. I was flabbergasted. This was not only something I had no control over, it was something no rational person could possibly have expected. What could I have done differently, asked the conductor to always seat my tours on the outside seat of every row on the train? It's ridiculous. At the most, this gentleman had to look past a couple of people, one of them his wife, to see the sights. It finally dawned on me that he didn't care. He wasn't going to be happy until he had complained to someone about it.

"What you need to do is stop back at the Tour Garden Desk right now and speak with the dispatcher working there. She will help you with your complaint and can get you on the next tour. Good luck."

I'm not used to being spoken to that way nor having a finger stuck in my face and could feel myself starting to tear up. I raised my crop, the signal for the guests to follow me, turned away from the still-sputtering gentleman, and beat a strategic retreat.

We could hear him still angrily voicing his displeasure to his wife and the other couple as the remainder of my tour group and I walked down the exit ramp and out onto Main Street. I have rarely had a tour begin any worse nor finish any better than that one. I was not the only person who realized how unreasonable his demands were. The rest of my people commiserated, were solicitous, and generally treated me like their favorite daughter for the remaining hours we spent together. Maybe they could read the shock and dismay on my face, but whatever the reason, they restored my faith in the decency of our guests.

When I finished a few hours later and returned to talk with Aquamarine about the man's complaint, she laughed.

"Yeah, that was ridiculous," she told me with a kind smile. "Don't worry, honey. We can't do anything about attraction boarding procedures. I put them on the next tour and told Citrine to be sure to give them a wide berth."

I let out a sigh. Even if the complaint *was* silly, it still hurt to be spoken to like that, and especially for something that was beyond my control. Later, Citrine debriefed me. They hadn't found anything Disneyland had to offer up to their lofty standards on the rest of the tour, either. They were apparently chronic complainers and generally unpleasant every step of the way. It had been a pretty miserable tour for her and the rest of her guests who had to listen to them whine about everything. Some people must go though life that way, I suppose, but it isn't fun to be around them. This is just one small example of why guides dreaded having people like them on a tour. Luckily for us, they were few and far between.

By the first summer I worked at Disneyland, I had studied Spanish for a total of five school years. High school Spanish and one year of college does not a native speaker make, but I was fortunate to be able to work with *la gente del mundo latino* who were so busy turning themselves inside out with joy to find a guide who could communicate with them that they glossed right over the many errors I must have been making every single time I opened my mouth.

The same could not be said for my friend, Diamond. She was an absolutely darling person, not a mean bone in her body, and deliriously happy to have such a great job. Instead of Spanish, however, she had taken five years of French. Now, as anyone who has studied a foreign language knows, that simply isn't enough for true proficiency. We memorized our eleven page spiels, we knew some specialized Disney vocabulary, but as far as being able to accurately converse with native speakers and maintain perfect use of however many verb tenses, that just ain't gonna happen.

I almost always managed to get by perfectly fine. My *grupos* were smiling and happy from the get go. I had them at, "*Buenos días, todos ustedes.*" They might even send up a happy cheer to hear their own language spoken. It was a marvelous confidence-booster. I could practice speaking with them under relaxing, pleasant circumstances. I didn't have to be concerned that someone would correct every misstatement, mispronunciation, or conjugation. That just wasn't done.

When I asked about something, they were delighted to offer assistance. They helped me to learn, to become a more proficient speaker. They gave me a lifelong empathy for the formidable hurdles to be overcome when anyone has to speak a language not their own. The majority of them, in fact, had a better grasp of English than I had of Spanish and were extremely gracious about offering help without being overbearing in the slightest. If you're nervous and afraid of making a mistake, it's awfully difficult to even want to say anything. That's the way Diamond described her French experiences that summer of 1970.

The French take their language very seriously, and by that I mean *very* seriously. There is an official board, one member for every letter of the alphabet, governing the correct use of words that are and are not acceptable like *le weekend* or *le hamburger*. Those would fall under the "not" category, I'm guessing. While French people themselves may well be wonderful and pleasant, they do tend to be language purists, at least those who visited Disneyland. Poor Diamond. While I was having a blast with my amenable Latinos, she would be quaking in her red knee socks that a French tour would show up at any moment. She actually hid in the rest room a couple of times, pulling her feet off the ground to avoid detection.

"Anybody seen Diamond? She's 'on' and there's a French tour getting ready to go." Aquamarine looked around the lounge, searching for the elusive French guide.

"I saw her, yeah," someone might vaguely venture, "but that was a little while ago."

"She might be doing something at the Magic Key Club."

"Oh, that's right," someone else might agree. "I know she's doing *something* right now."

Something such as hiding in the rest room.

No one would willingly give the poor girl away, especially if she had already led one difficult French tour that day. For a nickel an hour more than an English-only guide, it just didn't seem worth the aggravation. Speaking French for hours at a time with native speakers is a great way to improve your conversational skills, but not if you're scared *bleu* you'll make another mistake, and certainly not if everyone's just waiting to pounce on your every grammatical error and publicly correct you. That's no fun.

"You know what I've started saying before starting every French tour?" Diamond asked me one morning as we were getting ready.

"What?" We all knew by this time that she was seriously regretting the fact that she had ever admitted to being able to lead a tour in French.

"*Je parle français comme une vache espagnole.* It means: I speak French like a Spanish cow."

"Are you kidding? That's awful! Why would you say such a thing?"

"No, I didn't just make it up. That's an actual expression they use about someone who doesn't speak French very well."

"Oh, great. What a way to start out."

I told my Spanish-speakers, "I'll do my best, but please speak as slowly and clearly as you can to help me understand." My tours from Mexico, Spain, Spanish-speaking South American or Central American countries all encouraged me, helped me out when I faltered, and generally threw me a life preserver every time I was drowning. It sounded to me like some of Diamond's French groups threw her *le rock!*

One of my dearest friends, Kathryn, who passed away about a year ago, told me of traveling to France from her home in England while she was in high school. She had four years of high school French at the time. She went into a *boulangerie* and asked for *le pain*. Getting bread in a French bakery should hardly be an impossible task, but the person behind the counter acted as if she were completely unable to understand by giving that classic, Gallic shrug of her shoulders. Kathryn finally gave up. She is one of the most intelligent people I have ever known, and I've known quite a few. Academic merit scholarship to Oxford University smart. Doctorate at Carnegie Mellon smart. Head of Biomedical Statistics at the University of Iowa smart. You just can't make me believe she couldn't say "bread" after four years of studying French.

My adorable daughter-in-law Catherine, *une belle jeune femme*, is a French teacher. She has helped me come to realize over the years that certainly not all French people are as critical or demanding as those Diamond hid from in the tour guide rest room that summer. Catherine has lived and worked in both France and in Quebec, and she quite persuasively assures me that the majority of French-speaking citizens are just like people anywhere else, some kind, others critical. With her patient tutelage, I have come to understand that some of the impressions we had were perhaps unfair and that Franco-American interpersonal relationships have improved in the years since then. Let us hope so, at any rate. Cue *"La Marseilles."*

A strange occurrence, and one unfortunately not at all uncommon, happened when a group of Brazilians would approach the Tour Garden wanting to book a tour. There was just one tour guide, Emerald, who could speak Portuguese, and she didn't work seven days a week, so sometimes the guests from Brazil would be out of luck. Wanting to be helpful, however, the dispatcher working the desk would stick them with one of us Spanish language guides.

While Spain and Portugal may be neighbors, just like France and Germany, their two languages are, in fact, distinct. Just because you can understand one does not mean you can understand (much less speak) the other. A

French guide would never be given a group of Germans and told, "Just do your best." A Russian guide wouldn't hear, "Hey, Russia and China are somewhat contiguous, so I think you'll do okay understanding Mandarin. Good luck!" It just doesn't work that way, but that never seemed to discourage our eager-to-please dispatchers when it came to Spanish and Portuguese.

I have never seen an entire group of people any more gorgeous than those from Brazil. There was a song, popular at the time, that went, "Tall and tan and young and lovely, the girl from Ipanema goes walking...." Who knew that *all* Brazilians were tall, tan, young, and lovely? Clear, honey-colored skin, soft brown or black or sometimes hazel eyes, regular features, perfect physiques, waves of dark shining curls, warm smiles—they had it all. Prince Henry the Navigator must have taken with him on his voyages only the most heart-stoppingly gorgeous section of the Portuguese male population. What kind of recruitment posters were placed in the town square of Lisbon? Maybe something like:

Wanted: Handsome sailors ONLY.
No average-looking men need apply
for upcoming Voyage of Discovery.
Sincerely,
HRH Henry
(the Navigator)

When you'd walk into the garden and see a crowd of guests looking like they just stepped off the set of a telenovela, you could bet they were Brazilians. Grandma had calves of iron with buns of steel. Dad could melt a Mickey Mouse ice cream bar with his smoldering gaze. Mom just stepped from the pages of *Brazil Vogue*, her smile a dazzling benediction. The 2.5 kids were mini-versions of their parents. Honestly, how could one country be so blessed in the beautiful gene department? No idea, but despite their amazing looks, they couldn't speak or understand Spanish, and I couldn't speak or understand Portuguese.

As a result, there were lots of smiles and some comic charade-style pantomime. The riding crop got a workout pointing to various attractions, but in terms of any real exchange of information, not gonna happen. If you're going to spend up to three hours with a group of people, though, you could do a lot worse than spending them with delightful Brazilians.

The Brazilians were always groomed to within an inch of their lovely lives, but it became uncomfortably apparent to those of us leading guided tours that not every nation's people shared America's obsession with personal hygiene. Not everyone showers daily. Not everyone washes their clothes as frequently as we do. Not everyone finds deodorant a grooming essential. Don't get me wrong. This isn't a moral judgment, it's a fact of life.

You could argue that we waste an awful lot of soap and water and probably win that debate. Still, if you've ever walked by someone and were smacked in the face by the unmistakeable pong of body odor, you have just a tiny idea of what we sometimes endured. Not only that, I regret to say, but those who smelled the strongest also came from places where the concept of personal space didn't seem to exist in the same way it does here at home.

The more I tried to step back, the more surely but steadily they advanced. At times, in the extreme heat and the press of the crowd waiting in queues sometimes for as long as forty-five minutes at a stretch, it was practically impossible to take a breath. It was a crash course in getting to know folks of a different culture "up close and personal." The people themselves might be bright, friendly, and fun, but it was difficult to get past that pesky failure-to-be-able-to-breathe factor. It was one of the definite downsides of the job. Unless you've done it yourself, you simply can't fully appreciate the challenge.

The closest I've come to experiencing this situation in the intervening years is teaching an afternoon class full of adolescents who've just come from PE class. At least then I could say, as I took out a stick of Secret strategically placed in my top desk drawer, "Hey, people. Do you know what this is, 'cause I don't think some of you do! Please, don't come in here smelling to high heavens again!"

During the time I worked in the park, we entertained a seemingly endless parade of businessmen from Japan, and business must have been booming. We boarded the buses with a cheerful afternoon's greeting of *konnichiwa* or maybe an *ohayo* in the morning, and they were more than thrilled. Unfortunately, our greetings often unleashed a torrent of rapid-fire Japanese in response, to which we could only smile and nod. That was all we knew, other than *sayonara* at the end of the tour. Oh, and I knew that *gohan* meant rice, but that word didn't tend to come up much in casual conversation. There was a guide fluent in Japanese, but Jade was just one person. Like Emerald with the Portuguese–speaking guests, Jade couldn't possibly meet the needs of the deluge of her countrymen arriving frequently and in need of a Japanese-speaking tour guide. No, we all had to pitch in.

I, for one, loved taking Japanese tours. During my three summers, they were nearly one hundred percent male. The men wore business suits, white shirts, and conservative ties, and they tended to bow to us courteously, to which we bowed to them in return, to which they bowed once again. They were polite and extremely happy to see Disneyland at a time when Tokyo Disneyland was not even on the Disney drawing board.

Each one had an expensive, elaborate, difficult-to-operate camera on a strap around his neck. Some had two. A few had three, to the point where it was difficult for that person to remain entirely upright. Those Nikons and Canons weren't hanging there just for decoration, either. They got a real workout. I figured that I must have been nearly as common a sight as Mt. Fujiyama in many a Japanese photo album.

It soon became apparent that once was not enough. You posed with a group. One man snapped the picture, at which point he would rejoin the group and another man would serve as the group photographer. Each camera must be utilized. Each man must appear next to me. The combinations and permutations were executed with mathematical precision. Eventually, I could feel my face start to crack. My smile became a rictus. The men just kept rotating. Eventually, they had photographed the castle, each other, and me from every conceivable angle, and it was time to resume walking.

Uh, oh. Up ahead I can see the entrance to Adventureland, and it is looking decidedly photogenic. I hear from behind the rustle of twenty leather camera straps, the click of twenty shutter buttons, the twist of twenty F-stops being set, and here we go again. Smile!

An even more problematic, and ultimately legendary, situation arose one afternoon when a large contingent of Middle Eastern gentlemen had taken their tours and returned afterwards to the dispatcher desk in the front of the Tour Garden. Sometimes, when guides were waiting to leave with a tour group or simply waiting until charter buses arrived, they would line up in a row just outside the garden, looking every inch as pretty and sweet as a row of flowers.

As I've said, many of these girls were beauty pageant winners, gorgeous girls who would turn heads anywhere. They were the epitome of girls-next-door, dressed in cute little riding outfits. Oh, yes, and they were holding leather crops, too. Upon reflection, perhaps those were the source of some of the cross-cultural confusion.

"Hellooo," one of the men opened, approaching Aquamarine at the desk. Like Opal who worked over in Guest Relations, she had seen it all before. Well, almost all.

"Hello. I hope you enjoyed your tour of Disneyland," she smiled.

"Oh, yes, we enjoyed it very much. *Very* much. Now, we would like to book a more private tour."

"A more private tour?" Aquamarine was honestly perplexed. "We only have the one kind, sir. Do you maybe mean a VIP tour?"

"No, no, you don't understand." He smiled persuasively and indicated with an appreciative sweep of his hand the pretty line of now-eavesdropping guides standing in a red, white, and navy blue array. "We would like to have some of your tour guides come to our hotel tonight for a more *private* tour," he explained. "You see now?" He was hopeful.

For a moment you could have heard a golden riding-crop pin drop. Those were what we all wore on the ties of our white blouses.

"Oh, now I see," she admitted, after picking her jaw up off the desk where it had fallen. "Sir, we don't offer that kind of tour!"

"No?" He was crestfallen. The rest of the men's crests had also fallen. Oh, yes, they had most definitely enjoyed the tour and now wanted the good times to keep on rollin' back at their hotel.

How anyone could seriously think Disneyland tour guides were park hostesses by day and paid escorts by night was beyond ludicrous. How was it possible that a group of wholesome young ladies, each the very embodiment of the Disneyland Look, might be mistaken for ladies of the night? There were many witnesses to this legendary incident, all of whom couldn't wait to tell their colleagues about the "more *private* tour" they had managed to dodge that evening. Aquamarine was shocked to her core. I can still see her shaking her head in stunned disbelief.

"A private tour back at your hotel? I don't think so!"

It might very well be "a small world after all." We tour guides sat through the musical message of joy and peace and brotherhood among the children of "all the nations of the world" twice a day, practically every day. We non-native speakers made an enthusiastic effort to converse with our international guests in many different languages and dialects. We occasionally braved unpleasant guests, unpleasant odors, and unpleasant propositions.

The world might be small and getting smaller, but there were definitely some cultural sticking points still in evidence. Fortunately, though, for all of us who must share life on this little planet of ours, the good in people vastly outweighed the bad, the great majority of guests were delightful and appreciative, and the inspirational message of hope, peace, and happiness incessantly proclaimed by It's a Small World was one most people heard and heeded.

And so, for now, I bid you *adios, bon jour, sayonara, auf wiedersehen, tchau, ciao, ha det,* and a very fond farewell.

Hippies, Yippies, and Grand Floridians

"Everyone, get away from those windows—*right NOW!*" Garnet, the lead girl, ordered the rest of us. Fear colored her voice; she never spoke to us that way. "Lie down flat on the floor and be quiet." She locked the door to the tour guide office from the inside, but there was an awful lot of glass in the door and in those windows if anyone had been determined to break in.

"What's happening out...?" a guide began.

We hesitated, looking at Garnet, waiting for some kind of reasonable explanation. After all, we had never before been told to do anything even remotely like this before.

"Hush! You need to be quiet—*right NOW!*" she told us. "Lie down! We've been given orders by Security. I mean it!" No doubt that she meant it. You could hear it in her tone.

All of a sudden, this didn't feel like Disneyland; it felt like we were in some kind of a war zone. The mellow hippies and the more strident Yippies we'd seen milling about all day had somehow gotten themselves organized.

They could feel the day slipping away with nothing much having been accomplished. Their numbers were meager. Their protests, for the most part, fell on deaf ears. No national leaders in the movement were in attendance, if they had ever been involved at all. Once the Yippies managed to claim their little island situated in the middle of Rivers of America over in a back corner of Frontierland, what more was there to do? They could walk across the barrel bridge a couple of times and maybe smoke a few joints in Tom Sawyer's cave, both of which they did.

Now, however, things had escalated. That's how a group of tour guides ended up our workday lying flat on the floor, honestly frightened, and waiting for further instructions from Garnet.

We did as we were told. If you worked at Disneyland, that's what you did. It was part of the job. Phones continued to ring but mostly went unanswered. It was all we could do to stop ourselves from checking out what was happening right outside the office windows. People were quiet. Everyone, including me, was scared. This kind of thing was definitely uncharted territory. This all seemed very far away from the Happiest Place on Earth.

We were finally allowed to go back to the phone room and make personal calls if we needed to. I, of course, immediately called Ron. It wasn't the kind of conversation I had expected, not at all. He knew about the Yippie Pow-Wow plans, of course, but once he found out I was safe, he wasn't exactly sympathetic. He expected me to drive home by myself. He wasn't there and so he couldn't understand the palpable sense of tension and apprehension we felt.

At last, a serious but very kind team of Disneyland security guards came to escort us safely across Town Square. They took us in a couple of small groups so as not to attract too much attention. By then, however, no one was watching the tour guide office. All eyes were on the twin ranks of Orange County police officers clad in full riot gear lining both sides of Main Street. The conga line of Yippies had danced up the street and toward the castle by the time we were allowed to leave. Relief washed over us all as the Cast Members Only door shut firmly behind us with the protesters on the other side. We were safe, now, backstage.

Most people are familiar with hippies, even if they didn't personally live through the 1960s. It's difficult to convey the visceral reaction of shock and outrage average middle-class parents experienced when confronted with long hair, love beads, and peace signs. Not mine, however.

My Irish father managed to combine all three key elements into one memorable ensemble which he wore to surprise the neighbors one night. He took my long fall of hair, stuck it on top of his balding head, tied a bandana around it, and was instantly transformed from a pot-bellied, middle-aged dad into a pot-bellied, middle-aged hippie. He rummaged around, asking to borrow some of our long necklaces. He dubbed them "love beads," pulled several over his newly long hair, and headed across the driveway to the house of our neighbors next door.

Ding dong, ding dong.

He rang their doorbell while my mom and I waited for the hilarity to ensue from the safety of our porch.

Fred flipped on the light and opened the door.

"Peace, man." My dad raised two fingers, palm outward, giving Fred the peace sign. "Love, baby." Dad could barely manage to keep a straight face.

He could never look like anyone other than who he was—fun-loving Andy McGann. He must have felt as if he were completely incognito, a light-hearted hippie cruisin' by, spreadin' the love around, baby. He didn't take himself or the hippie movement too seriously. Fred, of course, guffawed uproariously. He was not only the perfect neighbor, he was the perfect good sport. Dad dredged up a few additional hippie-type comments he'd heard on *Laugh In* and then came home, delighted with himself. For the rest of the night, he kept giving us the peace sign.

It was a wild, psychedelic, black-lit extravaganza of a time. This was the birth of the generation gap, the "don't trust anyone over thirty admonition," free speech and free love, a time when political protests were the order of the day. Vietnam was the focus of many of these protests. If a guy didn't go to college, he went to Nam. Sometimes, he never came home. Draft cards and bras, too, were burned, and sometimes American flags.

My boyfriend Ron's draft number was 108 for his March 1 birthday. The government draft board drew everyone's birthdate one at a time, all 365 of them. My June 8 birthday was drawn 365th, a number wasted on me since only men were drafted. Number 108 meant Ron would most likely be called up if he didn't get into medical school, and the competition for grad school was a lot more high-stakes than it was getting a job at Disneyland.

He had to go downtown to Los Angeles to get a military physical. That made the whole thing seem terribly real. Because we were Baby Boomers, the competition for *everything* was absolutely fierce in a way people from other generations can't fully appreciate. We might not be the Greatest Generation, but we were certainly the generation with the greatest amount of competition from each other. The war, and opposition to it, were topics of nearly constant news coverage.

Hippies were, likewise, a hot topic in 1970. In addition to lots—and *lots*—of sex, hippie gatherings were usually accompanied by well-publicized drug experimentation, especially with LSD and marijuana. Harvard's Timothy Leary famously encouraged kids to "tune in, turn on, drop out" and was dutifully heeded by hoards of hippies. When they gathered *en masse* at rock concerts, as they did for three days on a remote dairy farm in Woodstock, New York, August 15 through 18 in 1969, history was made.

This isn't to say such pastimes as these were invented by people who came of age in the 60s, but because of the sheer number of teenagers who had been born after WWII, every trend we embraced took on a kind of momentous import, particularly in the popular press. Baby Boomers have always grabbed and held on with both hands to the microphone at the center of the national stage.

Not as many people remember much about the Yippies, a more radical offshoot of the hippie movement. In fact, when I mentioned this topic to a friend recently, she didn't even recall that there ever *was* such a term. Theirs was a far more political, less gentle ethos. Hippies went to San

Francisco strumming guitars and wearing flowers in their hair. Yippies went to Chicago with picket signs, angry chants, and a unique brand of outrageous street theater—and on one especially memorable summer day, they went to Disneyland.

Jerry Rubin and Abbie Hoffman, authors of *Steal This Book*, were two of the founders and best known of the Yippies. The name was said to stand for Youth International Party. Actually, its origin was a derivation from the media-created word hippie, from hip or hipster or the even older adjective hep. The word Yippie actually came before the founding of the Youth International Party, but regardless of which came first, the chicken or the egg, the Yippies were a rougher bunch than the hippies, more political, angrier, and more agenda-driven.

Perhaps their most notorious achievement was loudly disrupting the 1968 Chicago Democratic National Convention. They did their best to incite anarchy and eight of their number, later reduced to seven, were charged with criminal conspiracy and inciting to riot. Their seven-month trial was an extended field day for the national media, a legal three-ring circus, providing them with the forum they desperately coveted. Yippies were also great fans of elaborate pranks, sly humor, and theatrical antics. Most people may have largely forgotten about them, but not, I'll wager, those of us lying on the floor of the tour guide office that August 6, 1970. It was the day the Yippies decided to take over Disneyland.

Their plan was no secret. It was called the International Yippee Pow-Wow. They distributed hundreds of flyers with their entire, detailed, bizarre itinerary, most of which neatly fit their *modus operandi* of shock, humor, and theatrics. Familiarity with the the Disney characters might have been just a tad tenuous because one item on the imaginative list was a Porky Pig barbecue. The Yippies had run an *actual* pig for president two years ago, so their affinity with things porcine had already been established. They wanted to stick it to the man and to the pig, too, it seems. Unfortunately for them, Warner Brothers held Porky's contract, so barbecuing him wasn't in the cards.

Another one of their targets was Aunt Jemima's Kitchen, a favorite breakfast stop overlooking the Rivers of America and site of the annual tour guide breakfast. The Black Panthers were supposed to make an appearance there at 9:00 a.m. but didn't. Good thing, too, since the restaurant had been remodeled to become the River Belle Terrace by then. Aunt Jemima was nowhere to be found.

At some point, the female Yippies were supposed to liberate Minnie Mouse in Fantasyland from "male oppression." What they didn't realize, of course, was that underneath Minnie's flouncy, polka-dot dress they'd find a stogie-smoking little man. In retrospect, it's evident that most of the events were never actually intended to take place.

Just like the rest of the country, Disneyland management was familiar with the shambles the Yippies had managed to create at the Chicago Democratic National Convention. No way did they intend to allow those kinds of shenanigans to happen inside *their* berm, not if they had anything to say about it. As it turned out, Disneyland was far more organized and prepared that day than the Yippies were.

As many as a couple of hundred thousand Yippies were reported to be converging upon Anaheim from all parts of the country. Uh, not so much. That's many, many times more than the number of guests of the non-Yippie variety we ever expected on our busiest day. Only about 200 to 300 Yippies ever made it to the main gate on that ill-fated August day. Of those, it is estimated that perhaps no more than half had some kind of claim to being Yippies at all. The others were counter-culture kids out for some laughs and a good time, most either high or hoping to get that way as soon as possible.

The date chosen was no accident. It was the anniversary of the dropping of the atomic bomb on Hiroshima. Yippies, point taken, but nearly all of our fathers and uncles, and those of our friends and neighbors, had fought and bled, and sometimes died in the Second World War, so that point was quite a bit more complicated than it might otherwise have been.

In addition, the summer before my freshman year in college, Charles Manson's followers committed the ghastly, horrifically grisly murders that were still very fresh in the memories of those of us who lived close to Los Angeles. There wasn't a lot of local sympathy on offer for either the Yippie cause or for hippies as a group in 1970.

I got to work that day for my usual morning shift starting at 9:00 a.m. Management wasn't the only group prepared for the Yippie invasion. All of the tour guides and other cast members had been prepped about the day to come by our supervisors and were more than a little bit nervous about what we might expect. Rumors were flying, of course, between cast members. Then again, they always did.

There was the feeling of bated breath as we waited all day for something disruptive to happen. It didn't. There wasn't much of any kind of disturbance going on that day, and the 25,000-plus regular guests visiting us had a great time as expected. That was always our goal, and we did our best to make it happen every time we showed up for work. For some guests, this might be their first or their final visit, and we owed them a memorable experience. After all, we were grads of the University of Disneyland.

We took out morning tours as usual. It was, for the most part, a day a lot like any other, except for the fact that there were more security officers on duty than on an average day. Managers were also out in full force. You'd often see one or two strolling about, but that day you saw them on practically every corner of the park. Eyes darted back and forth as everyone seemed more watchful. It felt to me as if there were about twice as many people working in the park as would be typical.

Some people on the tours had heard, of course, about what might happen. The local news was hardly shy about covering this unprecedented event.

"Isn't today supposed to be Hippie Day or something?" a guest asked me. The finer distinctions between hippie with an "h" and Yippie with a "Y" eluded people even back then.

Other guests leaned in to hear what my response would be. There were clearly some clusters of non-traditional-looking young people hanging about doing their best to bolster each others' courage, and most of them kept trying hard to make it look as if something B-I-G was percolating. We had been asked not to engage with people about what *might* happen, so we mostly tried to keep things light.

"Yes, I've heard about that, too. So far, everything seems to be going pretty much as normal, though."

Smile. Walk. Keep smiling. Keep walking.

The guests were as curious as we were, but in 1970, it was not unusual to see kids with long hair, vacuous expressions, loudly patterned shirts, bell bottoms, copious amounts of facial hair (on the guys), and any manner of oddly mismatched accessories like beads, jewelry, scarves, and leathered or feathered hair ornaments. Fringe was also a big fashion statement.

When the hippie era first began, Disneyland refused to admit people who didn't meet some kind of informally "appropriate" dress code. In other words, just like the Disneyland Look, they knew it when they saw it. Definitely no long-haired guys. By the summer of 1970, it seemed long hair was here to stay and so the restrictions were substantially more relaxed. Hippies were allowed inside, even if not exactly welcomed with open arms. After August 6, 1970, however, those dress code restrictions were again clamped firmly back into place. That's what eventually led to the problem with the famous folk singer's date on our VIP tour in 1972.

Why had Yippies decided to invade the park in the first place? Accounts vary. Some say they wanted the park to be free for everyone to enjoy. Others claim it was to protest capitalism or even the Bank of America's support of the Vietnam War. Still others note the political nature of the protests and say the invasion was meant to shine a light on the many problems resulting from the war itself. It looked like the Yippies wanted to thoroughly disrupt the smooth operation of Disneyland, a place that was usually far removed from this kind of counter-cultural onslaught.

At lunch, we would hear from the guides doing area hostessing that the majority of the fun and games throughout that day had taken place in Fantasyland, a land we only saw obliquely from the back route leading to Small World. In my opinion, that is the same reason my hip VIP tour guests wanted to hang out there two years later. It is the childlike, innocent heart of the entire Disney mythos, and as such, it is the easiest, most vulnerable area to mock if you're so inclined.

Hippies and/or Yippies climbed up the rigging of the Chicken of the Sea Pirate Ship Restaurant, as many as forty of them, thus providing spectacular photo ops for the many professional photographers in attendance, but not much else was accomplished. The guests also took lots of photos of the theatrics to commemorate the memorable day. Up to this point, the scaling of the rigging was the most overt expression of any kind of "protest." What was being protested wasn't clear. Tuna sandwiches?

As the second tours started going out after lunch, the mood subtly started to shift. The sigh of relief we breathed at lunch might have been heaved too soon. Tension seemed to be mounting by the hour. Some of the security officers became increasingly agitated. Lots more discussions were going on over those headsets of theirs.

We didn't take tours anywhere close to Tom Sawyer Island, which had become the focus of a Yippee "invasion" when they decided to "take over" the island. They loaded up the flat, log rafts used to ferry guests to and from Tom Sawyer Island and packed themselves into Fort Wilderness. They became more aggressive and deliberately provoked confrontations with other guests. They ran the North Vietnamese flag up the flagpole and pulled down the Stars and Stripes that always flew over the cement-log fort.

Keep in mind that many of the otherwise average-looking dads walking around with their families had fought as young men in the European and the South Pacific theaters for that flag and the freedoms that came along with it. That was what they had done when they were about the same age as these Yippies. They were not about to stand idly by as this group of home-grown upstarts attacked the symbol of America.

The Yippies claimed their constitutional right to free speech and freedom of expression. To make the parallel clear, Abbie Hoffman himself had once dressed as a Revolutionary patriot during the infamous Chicago Seven trial. He had also worn a shirt made from American flag material and vowed something along the lines of, "I regret that I have but one shirt to give to my county," when he was required to remove it. The Yippies at Disneyland chanted in support of Ho Chi Minh, the Communist leader of North Vietnam: Ho-Ho-Ho Chi Minh, Ho Chi Minh is gonna win. They also chanted something about Teddy Kennedy, a reference to his culpability at Chappaquiddick, but the relevance of that chant is much less obvious. Both sides, tourists and Yippies, started shouting at each other.

About the time all this was going on, our late afternoon tours were just finishing up. We were bidding our guests good-bye, not suspecting that very soon the park itself would be completely shut down. It was becoming clear that something was up. Walking back though Tomorrowland and down Main Street, I was told repeatedly by the security guys I passed to "get back to the Tour Garden as fast as you can." It was located directly beside City Hall, across the street from the Bank of America, next to the Town Square, all of which would become targets of the Yippies' last stand inside the park.

No one was joking now. Everyone at work that day could see that something unprecedented was happening. Soon, a warning would be broadcast over the loudspeakers, speakers that had never been used for that purpose before, asking everyone to head for the main gate because Disneyland was closing early. Departing guests would be given re-admission vouchers.

By the time I got to the lounge, guides were milling around. No one was leaving. No one had any idea what had happened, but Lead Girl Garnet told us we were not permitted to leave the immediate area by ourselves under any circumstances. Something was going on just outside the tour guide building on Main Street.

Those of us just getting off work filtered out of the lounge, crowded together into the little tour guide office, and peered cautiously out the windows to see the action unfolding for ourselves. There was a long snake of people, some holding on to each other, yelling, jumping around wildly, and moving as a group up the street in the direction of Sleeping Beauty Castle. It was a very aggressive, scary-looking conga line.

All day long, people in management at Disneyland had been bending over backwards to diffuse the potentially volatile situation. Dick Nunis offered the groups of kids who showed up at the main gate ticket booths a discounted fifty-cent admission. They refused and paid full price.

Throughout the day, security officers repeatedly approached the small knots of Yippies hanging around. They said things like, "Be cool, guys. People are here to have a good time with their families."

It was the kind of calm advice hippies and Yippies received continuously throughout the course of the International Yippie Pow-Wow. They were treated to the same level of courtesy and service as any of our other guests. If anyone else had pulled stunts like smoking pot in the Journey Through Inner Space, climbing up the rigging on the Chicken of the Sea, or pulling down the flag on Tom Sawyer Island, they'd have been cooling their heels in the Orange County jail pronto. A lot was tolerated and overlooked that day.

There had been no official Disney push-back all day long; by late afternoon, it was time for them to make their move. One of the Yippies finally emerged as a leader and decided it was time to mobilize the troops. The protestors came together and headed for the Bank of America just inside the main gate. The rhetoric got angrier. Yippies became increasingly confrontational with security officers, with management, and with other guests. They had no intention of leaving that day without putting on some kind of a memorable display of strength and solidarity.

Word had been passed from one little group of them to another to converge on Town Square, and that's what turned into the long snake of gyrating Yippies we saw from the windows. One tried to hoist the Yippie flag up on a Main Street lamp post. It was black and red with a green marijuana leaf in the middle. Hey, why not? It had worked just swell when they hoisted the North Vietnamese flag over on Tom Sawyer Island a few hours before. They expected little or no resistance on Main Street. They were mistaken.

A big group of Disneyland guests spontaneously started singing "God Bless America." One of the men immediately ripped down the Yippie flag from the lamp post. A shoving match ensued. The luxury of hindsight makes their patriotic response an easy mark, but only twenty-five years had passed since the end of World War II. Its events were still etched vividly in the minds of those who had fought in it, those who had lived through it.

At last, Dick Nunis had enough. Placating them hadn't worked. Dick, cool-headed and a former USC football player, was justifiably concerned about the threat of violence and the potential that guests might be hurt. He gave an order. Suddenly, cast doors were flung open and some 150 Orange County police officers from Anaheim and Fullerton wearing full riot gear converged from backstage where they had been waiting onto Main Street. They carried bullet-proof, clear body shields, wore visored safety helmets, and carried clubs. Their presence was the swift, strong response made only after everything else had failed. The ratio of practically one officer per hippie/Yippie meant that the protest would be immediately shut down. No more Mr. Mice Guy.

That's when we tour guides found ourselves lying face down in the tour guide office on Main Street. It seemed like a very long time that we all lay quietly on the floor. The only thing you could hear from inside was the shallow breathing of girls and the intermittent ringing of telephones. There were lots of shouts and a roar noise coming at us from outside.

We would have to cross the Yippie-dense square in order to access the employee time shack, lockers, wardrobe, and parking lot. There was no way yet to get through the chaotic melee happening outside our windows. We waited. No cell phones existed, so there was no way to communicate with our families or friends. I wanted to call Ron and tell him to just *please* come get me. It was frightening, and I'd never before been seriously scared at Disneyland up until then. None of us had, I think.

When I finally did get to a phone, I was shocked when he told me he wouldn't come. "I've got an early shift and have to get to work first thing in the morning. Are you okay?"

"Yes." I paused. "I'm scared."

"But you're okay?"

"Yes. You *really* aren't going to come pick me up?" Maybe it was unreasonable to ask, but I didn't care at the time. I only knew I wanted him to come.

"Do you think you're okay to drive home?"

That was *not* the soothing reassurance I had hoped to hear.

"Yes. Bye."

"So call me when..."

I hung up.

By this time, Ron had been accepted into the University of California at San Francisco Medical School; he'd be leaving home in a little over a month. He hadn't said a single thing to me yet about where he thought our nearly year-long relationship was going.

This was the point that summer when the kids from Florida became, at least for me, the Grand Floridians. The Floridians had joined every department of Disneyland for on-the-job training during the summer of 1970 so they'd be ready to open Walt Disney World in 1971. Even the sweet and pretty English girl named Amethyst, Cicely's second-in-command, would be leaving Disneyland at the summer's end along with the rest of the Floridians. She had been a tour guide, a lead girl, and was next being promoted to head up the entire department of tour guides at Disney World. Our outfits were red, theirs would be blue.

My tour guide "little sister" Malachite was a quiet, beautiful girl with raven hair and milk chocolate skin. She was actually a few years my senior. Once we were allowed to get up off the floor, Malachite asked the rest of us if we wanted to join a bunch of the Florida kids for dinner back at their Anaheim apartment complex. Yes, we most certainly did. Security officers escorted us all across Main Street. Policemen in riot gear lined the sidewalks shoulder to shoulder, something I never expected to see. It felt tremendously safe and comforting to be able to leave as a group.

From the lockers we walked to the employee parking lot. In a couple of hours, the length of time it took for the police to empty the park, the lot would become the site of a last-ditch skirmish between the police and the ejected Yippies. In frustration, Yippies ripped out handfuls of flowers from the carefully tended beds and threw them at the police. Right. That'll fix 'em.

Standing at the gate leading to the employee parking lot was a tall, blond submarine pilot from Lakeland, Florida, one of several persistent guys who had continually asked me out all summer, even after I had made it repeatedly plain that I wasn't dating anyone but Ron.

"I just wanted to make sure you were okay," he told me. "Are you?" Deep blue eyes looked seriously into my green ones. His big hand rested lightly on my shoulder.

"We're going back to the apartment for dinner, Alan," Malachite told him. The Florida kids all knew each other and lived in an apartment complex not very far from the park.

He looked back at me. "Are *you* going?"

"Yes."

"I'll drive, then. I don't think you should be driving after everything that happened."

Thank you. That's *exactly* what I wanted to hear, but it wasn't the person I wanted to hear it from.

Grilled steaks, laughter, and time to relax and debrief about the crazy day with other guides did wonders for our jangled nerves. A good party with the gregarious Grand Floridians was just what we all needed. What I needed even more than that, though, was someone to care about how I felt.

"Will you come watch me when they hold the canoe races?" Alan asked me. "I think the subs have a shot at winning. You'd have to get up pretty early, though."

The races happened, I knew, in the early hours before the park opened. He smiled and put his arm around my shoulders as he walked me back to where the car was parked. It was late and getting chilly. Lots of us had to be at work the next morning.

The impromptu party began breaking up.

"Sure. I'll come."

Alan leaned down and gave me a quick kiss on the cheek. Was I breaking up, too?

"Great," he said. "See you tomorrow!"

I hadn't dated anyone else except Ron since we had met at the first dance of the college year, but when I was really scared and needed him to come get me, he hadn't. He was more worried about getting enough sleep. Okay, I *would* go to those stupid canoe races! Rah. Go, Subs. It wasn't like it was a proposal of marriage or anything. It wasn't even a date. It was just watching a bunch of cast members paddle the Indian canoes around Tom Sawyer Island, a tradition that happened every summer. My cousin, Matt, had done it back in his sweeper days.

Besides, Ron planned to take off for San Francisco at the end of the summer, probably wearing some flowers in his hair for all I knew. Everything between us suddenly felt very up in the air. No matter what happened, I'd always be grateful to the Grand Floridian who rescued me.

Did Ron and I work things out? We did. As with most guys, he had no idea how upset I had been by his choosing to be rational over choosing to comfort me. He was just being "logical." I was safe, and he was tired. Well, I hadn't been feeling the least bit logical when I called him. As it turned out, he didn't get a good night's sleep after all. He was up worrying about the situation and the way we had left things for hours. The next morning he called me—early. The way I had hung up the phone, he knew something was wrong. Both of us were upset. I was upset with him, and he was upset with himself.

Like all good boyfriends, he made the right call and apologized profusely—even if secretly, in his heart of hearts, he thought none of this was really his fault. He vowed he would *never* do anything like that again. (Well, let's face it, he could be pretty sure the Yippie invasion was a one-of-a-kind event.) He was as good as his word.

"I didn't realize how frightened you were, honey. I won't ever let something like this happen again," he vowed. "Tonight, I'm picking you up and taking you out for dinner so you can tell me all about what went on. It sounds awful. It was on the news."

"It *was* awful! You shouldn't have done that last night, you know." My voice broke.

"Yes, I know."

"...and I was *really* scared." At this point, I started crying quietly, and he could hear it.

"...and I am so sorry."

"Don't *ever* do it again." I took a shuddering breath.

"I know, I know. Believe me, I get it. So, I'll be there to get you after work tonight."

"Okay."

"I love you, you know."

"I know." *Sniff.*

I did go to watch Alan in the canoe races as I promised I would, but only as a friend. I thanked him for being there when I needed a safe shoulder to lean on, but I let him know that was all it was. He wasn't happy about it, but he also understood the situation with Ron. I had told him over and over that I had a boyfriend all summer, every time he asked me out. Alan just hoped that maybe last night had changed things. Who can say? If Ron hadn't called me that morning, it might have.

It was a narrow tightrope we walked throughout our relationship, but at the end of it all, striking that balance between logic and emotion was worth every effort we made to understand each other. He was rational, always thinking things through step by step. I learned to appreciate his thoughtful, calm appraisal of any situation. I was emotional, filled with joy and sadness and all the feelings in between. He came to understand and embrace the highs and lows along with me. Together, we made it through every crisis over thirty-eight years—starting with a Yippee Pow-Wow at Disneyland.

Ron and Andrea ... Happily ever after

12

Disneyland Information, May I Help You?

"Disneyland Information, may I help you?"

By the time I answered my first phone, I'd only been working at the park for a short time, a week or two at the most. I found myself sitting in a little room off the tour guide office filled with telephones, thick notebooks full of useful facts, and a handful of other tour guides, many of whom had worked at the park full time for years. I was in the deep end of the pool and treading water with no flotation device in sight.

"Yes, thank you. How late is Disneyland open on December 26?" my caller asked.

No, caller, thank *you*! That's exactly the kind of inquiry I felt very capable of answering.

"Disneyland is open from 8:00 a.m. until 6:00 p.m."

"...and what's the entertainment gonna be that day?"

The call had quickly become a lot more challenging.

I flipped to the entertainment section in the big notebook in front of me and searched for information I could tell my waiting caller. After all, I was supposed to be Disneyland Information. For each day of the month, the notebook listed special entertainment acts, along with performance times and venues. In addition to these short-term musical acts, there were always the regular shows that went on daily, such as the Christmas parade and several Disneyland bands and dancing and singing groups. This was something I could put my fingers on relatively quickly. Not everything was that easy.

Now, whenever I'm the victim of a dropped call, I have a better understanding about how easy it is to do that when you only meant to put someone on hold or transfer them to another department. Oops! Going, going, gone. No way to call them back, either, because caller ID was not available. It isn't as simple a job as you might imagine to think, talk, search for, and share information simultaneously. It has made me more patient when I'm dealing with telephone operators ever since. If you've never had to do it yourself, don't be too hard on the person on the other end of the line.

When there were more tour guides than there were tours for them to lead, we would rotate through a variety of other tasks, some more frustrating and difficult than others, but for me nothing was as scary as the phones. By the summer of 1972, I wasn't nearly as overwhelmed as I had been on my first few times during the Christmas holidays in 1969, but I never felt completely at ease. By 1972, however, I knew far more about the inner workings of the park and felt fairly confident picking up the receiver.

"Disneyland Information, may I help you?"

"What's the entertainment on this Saturday ... oh, and how late are you open?"

Easiest thing first. I told them park hours, which I knew by heart, and then looked up the special entertainment.

"Helen Reddy is appearing onstage at the Tomorrowland Terrace and Tex Beneke (BEN-uh-key) and his band will be playing on the Plaza Terrace." Whew. Nailed it.

"Who are they?"

That was more difficult to answer. *Pete's Dragon*, a Disney film starring Helen Reddy as the mom, would not come out until 1977. All I could think of was "I am woman, hear me roar...." It had been released in 1972 and was highly popular at women's liberation conventions and was often played on the radio. That was her signature song, an anthem of the movement.

"Helen Reddy is an Australian. She wrote and sings 'I am Woman.'"

"Oh." The disappointment was palpable. "Who's Tex Beneke?"

More frantic flipping through the pages of the big notebook, madly trying to find out something, anything, to share about Tex. Since I didn't want to drop the call and had given up trying to manage the "hold" button (which should have realistically been marked "drop" on any phone I had the misfortune to answer), I held my hand over the speaker and whispered the question at large to anyone in the office who wasn't currently having a telephone conversation.

"Does anybody know who Tex Beneke is?"

"Big Band," came the cryptic, whispered answer from one of the full-time girls.

"Big Band?" I repeated softly.

She nodded.

"Big Band," I said into the phone quietly and tentatively.

"Big Band?" my caller echoed.

"Yes, Big Band."

Now, years later, I know that Tex Beneke had been a famous member of the Glenn Miller Orchestra during the Big Band era of the 1930s and

1940s. It was the 1970s, but Tex was still going strong on his sax. I eventually came to love those old songs from my parent's generation like "In the Mood," "Little Brown Jug," and the alliterative "Chattanooga Choo Choo." Back in 1972, however, I was clueless about it.

About a decade after I'd led my last tour, Mr. Beneke appeared on a television commercial selling an album of oldies but goodies and singing a few lines from his famous hits. I nearly fell off the couch. Tex!

"Ron, that's Tex Beneke!" What an exciting moment. Yes, by this time we'd been married about ten years.

"Who's Tex Beneke?" my husband asked, looking up from his newspaper without a great deal of interest.

"Big Band."

"Big Band?"

"Yes. Big Band."

Another task we might be assigned when we weren't leading a tour was far more fun than phones and less stressful. It was called area hostessing and was never a chore. Basically, we just had to stand in an area in one of the lands and answer questions. It was a chance to circulate through areas of the park we seldom saw and to meet people other than those wearing riding caps and carrying crops.

"Where's your horse," I'd hear from someone for the thousandth time.

"I don't know, but if you see him, please let him know where I am!"

One of my favorite spots to area hostess was New Orleans Square because of its many cool stores where I could surreptitiously window shop. Everything was new and gorgeous. I made mental notes of which ones to visit later on Date Nite. The architecture with its many wrought iron embellishments was beautiful, but it often elicited comments like this:

"It doesn't really look like this, you know," a passing guest would stop to inform me, as though I had personally managed to flub the realism.

"Oh?" I'd inquire as politely as if I'd never heard that observation before.

"No, the streets in New Orleans are straight and these are curved."

"That's interesting. I've never been there, but it sounds lovely." I'd give them a smile. "I hope I can see if for myself one day."

People loved to share things about places they know as well as we guides knew Disneyland. They were proud, and justifiably so. What I heard thousands of times more than that observation, however, and I heard it wherever and whenever I happened to be area hostessing, was this:

"Where's the nearest bathroom?"

It's funny how many times we were asked to point out the *nearest* restroom, as though without that key qualifier, we might be tempted to send them to a restroom many lands away.

"Where is the rest room?"

"*¿Donde está el cuarto de aseo?*"

The Loo. *Die Toilette.* Water closet. *Les toilettes.* We heard restrooms called lots of things.

It was usually fairly easy to deduce what people meant by the rising level of desperation in their voices, regardless of the language they were speaking.

Most of the Disneyland restrooms are not exactly placed front and center. They're available if and when you need them, but they are meant to fade tastefully into the background. I soon learned where even the most tucked-away toilets were located. When I was an undergrad at University of Disneyland, we were told to always be very specific about giving instructions to the restrooms because if you weren't, misunderstandings could occur.

Our instructor told us about one busy cast member on Main Street who had given the following answer when asked by a child where the nearest restrooms were located: "You just go behind the Flower Market."

He did.

The child had taken the instructions quite literally. He didn't realize that there were actual rooms for the purpose back there. He just "went."

Area hostessing gave us a chance to check out other break areas. That's when I met the feisty Pinocchio in Fantasyland. It's also where I kept running into a friendly sub pilot named Alan. The most unusual break area, and one I spent quite a bit of time using on hot summer afternoons, was located in Adventureland. That was always such a nice spot to be. Lots of shady foliage, two main destinations which were located right on the only thoroughfare, and an interesting mix of foot traffic. Most people were looking for the Jungle Cruise and the Swiss Family Treehouse.

All you needed to do was give them the two-finger point and tell them to keep walking. No possible way to go wrong. Guides came by with their tours. If a supervisor was prowling through the park, they'd spread the word. Jungle Cruise skippers could always be counted on for a good laugh, and the Tahitian Terrace had tropical background music to add to the mood.

Up a back stairway above the Tiki Juice Bar and Sunkist I Presume, (no, seriously, that's what it was called), you'd find a large, darkened room equipped with a bed and couches and chairs. Best of all, it was air conditioned. The heat was intense in the summers, and our costumes were not at all suitable. We were like those British colonialists of the previous century who steadfastly dressed for England's damp, cool climate regardless of where in the world they happened to find themselves.

Forty-five minutes on, fifteen off. That was a lot more "off" than we ever had on our tours. As far as I knew, no one ever used that Adventureland break room but us. At least I never ran into anyone else there. You could be assigned to do a lot worse things than area hostessing when you didn't have a tour to lead. One of those things was working the MKC, the Magic Kingdom Club.

The club itself was fine. What was less appealing was the tedium of doing the clerical tasks it required of us. People could "join" the club and get books of tickets good for any attraction in the park. A Magic Key ticket would get you on all the most popular attractions as well as admittance to the park. It was an excellent value. Employees at hundreds of companies in southern California received membership cards, including my mom who worked at Triple A. It was a forerunner of the kinds of discounted deals you can qualify for today if you frequently patronize a particular hotel chain or eat at a certain restaurant. MKC also published a nice little magazine about Disneyland. It was good business for the park and a perk for local employees.

"We need two volunteers to go over to MKC," Aquamarine said, poking her head through the door to the lounge where Diamond and I were finishing lunch.

We were the only two in the room.

"Looks like you found them," I told her. Dispatchers knew there was only one guide who loved going over to the MKC, and that was because she had a thing for one of the guys who worked there. Tourmaline, in fact, had a thing for many guys. After a while, they quit sending her over at all.

We headed across Main Street, through the cast door, and toward the administration building on our way to the little office where we'd be crammed for the rest of the afternoon. Neither of us liked it, but it beat going home early with fewer hours.

Time drags when you're not doing a job you enjoy. Tours were over in the blink of an eye. It was the same with teaching. When you were busy teaching, the days flew by. On "teacher work days" (as though there were some other kind), when we stayed at school and the students didn't, time stood still. There was one teacher, however, who said without the slightest understanding of the irony in her statement, "I always get so much more done with no students around." For me, office work made me feel like the hands on my Mickey Mouse watch had stopped moving entirely.

"You'll be doing envelopes," we were told brightly by a receptionist who worked the desk.

Be still, my heart.

She handed us each a box of maybe three hundred envelopes, all of which needed to be stuffed, stamped, and sent. This was when I learned to appreciate the benefits of leading tours. Being outside with guests was just about always a pleasure with very few exceptions. Being inside with envelopes wasn't. While it was always fun to chat with Diamond, the work itself was not only mindless, it was mind-numbing. It made me realize how very little I wanted to do office work.

"I'm breaking up with John," Diamond said quietly after we'd stuffed about half of our assigned quota of envelopes. "I haven't told him yet."

"What happened? I thought you two were practically engaged!" I was genuinely surprised. They seemed like the perfect couple; they'd been dating for years. I'd met him a few times, and he always seemed like such a nice person.

"We were, yeah, but there are so many great guys working here...." Her voice trailed off.

"Are they as great as John?"

"That's just it. I don't know. I want to be able to date lots of guys. Besides, John isn't very exciting."

I knew exactly the exciting kind of guy she meant: Tyler. He was most assuredly smokin' hot, and because he worked on Pirates, we usually saw him twice a day, every day. He was crushing on Diamond and kept asking her out. She was as sweet as she was pretty, a nice girl in every way.

There's no doubt about it, it was flattering. Several guys in the park showed me that kind of attention, but I was in a serious relationship and told them so. There was Alan, a tall, blond guy from Florida at Disneyland for the summer who worked on the Submarine Voyage, one persistent blond skipper on the Jungle Cruise, and one really cute operator on Pirates (not Tyler—he was so obviously a player, and that was the kind I always avoided). In fact, it got so bad with a guy in Wardrobe that I'd have someone else exchange my costume for a fresh one so I wouldn't have to go to the window when he was working. Every few minutes, you'd run into some adorable cast member looking for love. Tour guides were moving targets. See why everyone wanted to work at Disneyland?

One Date Nite, Ron and I rode Pirates and happened to run into Tyler working a night shift.

"Ron Keech! How ya doin', buddy?" Tyler asked, smiling. "Didn't know you were dating a tour guide, Ron." He nodded at me.

"Hi, Tyler. You guys know each other?"

"Yeah, we went to school together," Ron told me. To Tyler, he said, "We've been going out nearly a year. So, what's going on with you?"

"Still at Cerritos. Thinking about switching to Cal State Fullerton. You?"

"Going to med school in September. UCSF."

"Yeah? No kidding? Good for you!" Tyler was surprised and happy. He later told me how much he admired my boyfriend when they were in school together and always asked about Ron when he saw me afterwards.

"Well, see ya," Ron called as our boat arrived at the loading dock.

He told me that he had met Tyler at Cerritos JC but hadn't seen him for about two years. He had been in a couple of Ron's pre-med classes but apparently hadn't done very well. Ron had recently been accepted to UCSF Medical School and was still over the moon about it. Tyler had switched from biology to photography and was now considering switching to yet another major, according to Diamond.

"He was popular, especially with the girls, but I never thought he had much of a work ethic," Ron told me once when we were on a boat drifting past the Bayou.

"I don't think he's changed all that much," I said.

Back at Cerritos Junior College, when the two had some courses together, the school had just opened and their classes often had to be held in temporary trailers. Ron was taking twenty semester hours at a time, making straight As and working twenty hours a week as an assistant manager at McDonald's. He knew something about a work ethic. In fact, his work ethic was an issue that came between us at times. He was so driven that he sometimes didn't know how to relax or take time off—or when he should have come picked me up the day the Yippies took over Disneyland.

After graduating from Cerritos, Ron had transferred to Occidental College where we met at "The Hustle", the first dance of the school year. He was a senior and I was a freshman.

During a break, I asked him his name. The music was deafening.

"Juan Kleek," he said.

"What?"

"*Juan Kleek!*" he repeated, shouting into my ear this time.

That's funny, I thought. He doesn't look the least bit Latino. Blue eyes, brown hair, and a skin tone that he would later call frog-belly white. The next day I received a telephone message in my mailbox saying I'd missed a call from Ron Keech. Oh, *that's* what he said.

Even though the tuition and expenses were considerable and required him taking out student loans, getting personal recommendations from professors who knew him well would be essential when applying to medical school. That wasn't something he could count on at a huge university.

After he read Albert Schweitzer's autobiography in eighth grade, Ron decided he wanted to become a doctor. I've never known anyone in my life before or since who worked nearly as hard. Most of his high school friends quit before graduating. His best friend was dead within a year of dropping out. Until his senior year in high school, Ron played varsity football (Freeway League champs), played lead guitar on his Fender Jazzmaster in his rock band, and played around in his classes. Then, it dawned on him that if he wanted to practice medicine, he'd have to buckle down—and soon.

He didn't have academic role models at home. Neither of his parents ever graduated from high school. They met while working at the Salvation Army in Little Rock, Arkansas, and fell in love. They were married immediately following his mother's last day of ninth grade. She had just turned fifteen. Ron's older brother was born the following June after the family moved to southern California. His dad was seventeen and worked in an aluminum factory in Tustin. His parents were married over fifty years before his father passed away.

Once Ron flipped the switch in his academic life from off to on, he never faltered in his single-minded commitment. Eventually, he graduated from Occidental, Phi Beta Kappa, and became an eye surgeon and professor of medicine at one of the most highly ranked ophthalmology programs in the United States. After his death in 2007, a professorship in pediatric ocular genetics was endowed in his honor. He had come a long way. You may have heard it said of George Bush that he was born on third base but thought he hit the triple. Following that analogy, Ron was born in the stadium's parking lot and managed to hit a home run.

As far as I was concerned, my friend Diamond was making a big mistake dropping John for Tyler. John was steady where Tyler was flashy. John was sincere where Tyler was smooth. John did well in school where Tyler was far from a stellar student. She had already made up her mind, though. John didn't stand a chance.

Tourmaline, an experienced tour guide had once warned our training class with considerable confidence, "If you think you can remain engaged at Disneyland, you can't. Forget it. I was engaged when I was hired and it lasted about two weeks. This place is crawling with gorgeous guys. You can't pick just one!"

She was undoubtedly the most experienced guide in many ways. When I'd shadowed her once in training, she acted more like a contestant on *The Dating Game*, a popular television program, than someone leading a guided tour. Instead of one bachelorette having to choose among three bachelors for a date like the premise of the show, this was more a case of one bachelorette dating an infinite number of Bachelors.

"Hey, Tourmaline, whatcha doin' Friday night?" A handsome RETLAW guy immediately came over and asked her out as soon as we boarded the train.

"What time Friday night?" came her snappy retort. "Get in line!" This was delivered with a sweet smile as our train pulled away from the Main Street station.

She wasn't kidding. Her social calendar was always booked solid. No matter where we went in the park, some good-looking, eager ride operator would call, "Tourmaline, wait!"

"Sorry, gotta go!" And with that, she was off to the races.

She was cheerful and adorable, tiny and flighty, self-absorbed and vain. She made no claims to the contrary. For Tourmaline, the park was one enormous buffet table filled with a wide array of tasty dishes, and she was perpetually famished. She couldn't pick just one—they were all so yummy. She was having a great time, living fast and fancy-free, and she honestly didn't see how anyone else could possibly remain faithful to only one guy. Her ex-fiancee had undoubtedly saved himself an expensive divorce.

We eventually finished stuffing those hundreds of envelopes for the MKC. The afternoon, as predicted, dragged interminably, just as it always did when you weren't actually leading a tour. It was slightly better than answering phones and a lot worse than area hostessing. Luckily, we spent the vast majority of our time doing what I loved best, leading tours.

Diamond and Tyler dated for the rest of the summer. They made a gorgeous couple. Maybe it worked out after all. Maybe Tyler settled down and quit being such a consummate player. Maybe he switched to Cal State and chose a major he could manage. Maybe he finally managed to graduate from college. Maybe they got married and lived happily every after.

Yes, and maybe those are the Three Little Pigs I see flying over Fantasyland.

Ghosts of
Attractions Past

Have you ever had the experience of returning to your home town after a long absence? It can be disconcerting. You find some of the old things are still there, but the familiar buildings of memory have undergone a good deal of updating over the intervening years. Maybe just a fresh paint job, different window treatments or trim, or here and there something entirely new might have sprung up in a formerly empty lot. Things don't look quite the way you remember them. That's how it is with Disneyland and me. I see it in my mind most clearly as it was from 1969 to 1972 when I worked as a tour guide, but the ghostly shadows of the Disneyland of my childhood are there, too. Things may change, but they never entirely vanish from memory.

There was once a big earthquake with its epicenter squarely in the middle of my southern California home town. Until it happened, earthquakes were minor annoyances. The 1906 San Francisco temblor was so long ago that we barely remembered California quakes could be deadly. Hanging lamps swayed, water in a pool or bathtub might wash back and forth, the drapery cord on windows at school would swing gently, or you'd get that odd sinking-elevator sensation in the pit of your stomach and know one had just happened.

There hadn't been anything seismically notable in our little corner of the state since the Tehachapi quake on July 21, 1952, when the crib I was sleeping in bounced across the bedroom floor and hit the wall on the other side of the room. In fact, small quakes and quivers were so common that I quickly tired of the reliably loud and gleeful announcement from several boys in my elementary class, "It's *Andrea's* fault," whenever we experienced a minor tremor during school hours. For those of you unfamiliar with the Pacific Ring of Fire, we sat atop the volatile San Andreas Fault. It frequently let us know that, and even though it hadn't jarred us loose into the ocean just yet, it remained a force of nature to be reckoned with.

When an earthquake hit my home town, the destruction came as a serious shock. Modern brick facades of the 1950s and 60s turned into piles of debris jumbled in the middle of the streets. It was dumbfounding to find that beneath their formerly sleek, updated exteriors, the familiar businesses downtown had begun their lives *way* before mine. Ornate wood carvings and nineteenth century architectural curlicues graced the old storefronts. The curtain of time was pulled back, and everyone caught a brief glimpse of the town as it had appeared when it was built. Those sturdy old buildings stayed firmly in place, while their newer surface updates cracked, crashed, and tumbled down around them. The violent changes happened in an instant.

Changes at Disneyland happen over the course of years, and they happen with a good deal of prior planning. Constant transformation was always Walt Disney's intention. Disneyland was meant to grow and change, and so it has. Yet when I see the park today, I can still see lingering ghosts of the old Disneyland, the way things used to be. Much-loved attractions, a few not loved at all, and iconic landmarks may be gone, but they will never be forgotten.

When we disembark these days from the *Mark Twain*, I can't help looking to the left where Thunder Mountain rises. Through the mists of passing years, I can almost see (and smell) the original Mule Pack attraction. From 1955 to 1956, the trusty mules gave us rides a lot tamer than the modern roller coaster that eventually replaced them. It was the only chance we suburban kids had to get anywhere near anything equine. At first, the premise was fairly primitive, just a string of laid-back mules ambling through the simulated desert, a yet-to-be-developed seven acre parcel in a corner of Frontierland near the Circle D Corral.

The desert isn't all that difficult to simulate in southern California. Most of the lower half of the state only blooms at all because the Colorado River was diverted to allow us golf courses, green lawns, and the lush, insatiably thirsty landscaping of Disneyland. At first, the mules walked through relatively barren rocky outcroppings and grassy hillocks. It was one of the original attractions when the beautifully mature plantings you see today were still very small, simple, and decidedly plain.

By 1956, funds had been earmarked to improve the Mule Pack experience. With the improvements came a new name. The attraction became known as the Rainbow Ridge Pack Mules. A tiny Western town dubbed Rainbow Ridge was added. It was a lot cheerier and brighter than the real thing they had over at Knott's Berry Farm. (Walter and Cordelia Knott purchased and transported actual California desert ghost-towns to their theme park.) The name Rainbow Ridge Pack Mules lasted until 1960 when it was changed yet again to the Pack Mules Through Nature's Wonderland.

As you rode through the man-made wonderland, you'd see a coiled rattler ready to strike beside the trail, the tip of its tail mechanically going back and forth like a little metronome. There were some rough-looking coyotes, mountain goats, and a puma perched on simulated cliffs and boulders. Their tails, too, jerked rhythmically back and forth. Occasionally, a predator's neck would swivel, its jaws snap. Tiny heads of prairie dogs or a jackrabbit's long ears might slowly rise from their burrows and then slowly sink back down. A small, reliable geyser spouted from the sand and colorful pools of "mud" bubbled. The bubbles were created by pumping air into the pools, not geothermically like the Yellowstone ones they imitated. On the plus side, ours didn't come with the realistic stench of sulphur.

These improvements upon nature were created before Disney's Imagineers had perfected the concept of audio-animatronics, before the moment Mr. Lincoln would rise, somewhat Lurch-like, from his chair to astound us.

Strategically placed wooden crates stenciled with DANGER or TNT, a few shovels, pick-axes, and other tools of the miner's trade dotted the trails. Nothing high-tech here, only the muted clop of the hooves of the mules hitting the soft earth and the creak of well-worn saddle leather. It was such a simple concept, but that's part of the charm that made it so special.

For just those few minutes, sitting astride one of the large, lumbering Disneyland mules, I could imagine myself cantering briskly over the verdant English countryside clad in smartly tailored jodhpurs and jacket, sailing blithely over jumps on a challenging steeplechase course just like Mouseketeer Annette did in "The Horsemasters" on *Walt Disney's Wonderful World of Color*. Once, I even sat on a sawhorse in my backyard with a Tupperware bowl upended on my head like a riding cap. Yes, I was *that* desperate. Apart from the mules, that's the closest I ever got to riding. I loved every single minute of each mule ride I ever took, even if we never moved at a gait faster than a plodding shuffle.

What I failed to realize, however, was that the mules were not *always* placid. In fact, occasionally, they could be downright dangerous.

People are called mulish or mule-headed or stubborn as a mule for good reason. A mule is a cross between a male donkey and a female horse. While usually strong and stable on its feet, it be a decidedly dicey mount. Mules will sometimes inexplicably stop dead in their tracks, plant all four feet firmly on the ground, and refuse to budge a step. Occasionally, they will buck a rider off. Very occasionally, they might even subsequently roll on top of that same rider, and so it was with the string of Walt Disney's mules.

Records show that as many as a dozen lawsuits were filed against the unreliable mules over the years, and each one of them resulted in a loss for Disneyland. This was shockingly unprecedented at a time when the park's legal juggernaught won practically every suit of *any* kind brought against it.

One immensely popular book you've very likely already read reveals the "inside story" of the park. It tells of a woman who brought a successful lawsuit because she was bucked off and rolled on by "an 8,000 pound mule" at Disneyland. I'm not entirely sure if that number was merely a typo, an exaggeration by the woman's attorney, or simply an incorrect transcription from the original text of the lawsuit. An 8,000 pound mule would be roughly the size of an adult female Asian elephant.

Imagine, if you will, a sedate string of normal-sized mules waiting patiently in line for their next group of riders to mount. Their tails lazily flick at flies, their long ears twitch. Each of them would weigh approximately 800 to 1,000 pounds. 1,200 pounds would be one *big* mule. Just like the row of guests ready to ride them, the mules would be standing in sequential order from smallest to largest.

Then, imagine your eyes being drawn inexorably to the very last mule in line, a veritable colossus of a mule, a mule standing eight feet tall at the shoulder, the height of an average ceiling, with a gargantuan bulk literally the size of an elephant. I don't know about you, but I wouldn't want *that* one rolling on me, either. An 800-pound mule would be plenty bad enough, but an 8,000-pound mule would have made the Trojan Horse look like a Shetland pony.

Cousin Matt, several years before he became a sweeper, rode the mules with me one summer. He was in high school by then and sat a few mules behind me in the line. His mule got a little frisky and began playfully crowding the one standing in front of it. The mule skinner barked some kind of command. Gee? Haw? I can't remember just what it was, but it didn't matter because Matt's single-minded mount paid no heed. It keep crowding its neighbor until finally Matt's new Converse white sneaker was wedged gently but firmly up the rear end of the mule standing directly in front of his. We had yet to begin our slow shamble out of the boarding pen when a cry of real anguish arose from the back of the mule train.

"*ARGHHH!* What the *heck*?" Matt cried. He was clearly distressed about something.

"What's the matter back there, son?" the wizened old mule skinner turned from his seat in the front of the pack to inquire. His face was a map of wrinkles, as tan as the saddle leather upon which he sat.

"A mule just crapped on my foot, that's what's the matter!"

By this time, we could smell the unmistakeable odor of fresh, green mule dung.

"Can't be helped, son. *Hy-y-y-ah*," the skinner gave the giddy-up signal and we were off.

For the remainder of the day, unfortunate Matt squished along with one white and one green sneaker, smelling like a wrangler just back from a hard day on the Circle D. Did he sue? Of course not, but I can understand why eventually the mules were consigned to their place in the pantheon of attractions of the past. Too many mishaps, too many lost lawsuits, and perhaps one legendary mule so big it beggared belief.

Another attraction of the past was the Flying Saucers. These lasted from 1961 to 1966, and as far as I was concerned, that was five years too long. I have no nostalgic memories of them as I do of the mules. The attraction consisted of a fairly large semi-circular area covered with round circles dotting its surface. Once the time limit for your turn was up, all of the white, aerodynamic saucers would be corralled back into an area beside the line for you to exit while new people could board. There were two sets of round saucers, so that while one set was gliding smoothly along on a cushion of air, guests on the others were being unloaded and the saucers reloaded. Loading guests was a slow, labor-intensive process. That was usually the kiss of death for a Disneyland attraction.

Columns of air were pumped with a good deal of force up through the disks which would open when their sensors detected the presence of a saucer. Once you boarded your saucer, you were treated to the illusion of flight by rising above the ground, even if by only a couple of inches, and being propelled forward. There were small handles, one on each side, that you used to guide your vehicle around the interior of the enclosure. The saucer should theoretically move in the direction you leaned. One passenger per saucer meant a substantially long wait. Orange safety bumpers were there to prevent any serious collisions. It looked like all kinds of reasonably harmless fun to me when it was new and I was nine.

After waiting for what seemed a long time, I was at last ushered onto my very own saucer. The ride operators gave us the go-ahead and we were off!
They were off.

My saucer stayed firmly in place. Instead of rising on a floating cushion of air, mine appeared to be sucked down firmly to the surface. All around me, the other saucers bounced and bumped and "flew" gaily back and forth across the field of disks.

One of the operators came over to where I sat and attempted to dislodge my recalcitrant saucer from the maw of a stubbornly sucking vortex. I can't remember if he attempted to dislodge it with his hand or foot or if he had some kind of specialized tool designed expressly for the purpose. I seem to recall a long pole, similar to one that might be employed for punting on the Thames, but that might be fanciful. All I know for certain is that my saucer didn't budge, not one little disk.

I had waited in line, surrendered my ticket, and sat in an immobile saucer until the ride was over. There might have been some minimum weight limit

I didn't quite make. You were supposed to shift your weight to direct the saucer. Was it that I just didn't understand the concept of what I needed to do? Was my saucer truly unlucky, defective in some way? I never had the nerve to try again. Historically, this ride caused many headaches for the operators. Regardless of the reason, I was relieved to see them go.

A Tomorrowland landmark I do miss is the Monsanto House of the Future, which opened in 1957 and closed ten years later. It was meant to depict a prototypical house in the year 1986. My family, friends, and I all loved walking through the four protruding pods, the living spaces of the house. It resembled a four-leaf clover rising up from a sturdy stem. I remember a great many of daily life's necessities springing forth at the touch of a button and then retracting once they had served their purpose. Like the Brady Bunch in their house that would make its appearance in 1969, who needed to ever be confronted with the esthetically unpleasant sight of a toilet?

The house's exterior was white, and the warm glow from the lights inside made it look simply gorgeous at night. It seemed to float. Things we gawked at like electric toothbrushes, dishwashers, and microwave ovens, once "space age" technology, have become commonplace. The furnishings could fit comfortably with no modifications whatsoever into any modern house, apartment, or condo.

One of the main products showcased by Monsanto was plastic. Calling something "plastic" is now pejorative; it's a derogatory term that hints at something inauthentic and cheap. This house was far from that. The House of the Future was a genuinely cozy place that George, Jane, Judy, and Elroy Jetson would have found quite comfortable, the Buzz Lightyear equivalent of the clever Swiss Family Treehouse. No need for Rosie, the robot maid, however, as it practically cleaned itself. Most of us would have gladly enjoyed the many creature comforts it had to offer.

The house eventually got its sweet, sweet revenge. Times change, of course, and with them our notions of what the future might hold. When it was at last decided to demolish the no-longer-quite-so-futuristic abode, the house itself was having none of it. It seemed that nothing short of an incendiary device of epic proportions could destroy the plucky little plastic domicile.

It calmly withstood a wrecking ball. Disney alum Miley Cyrus could have identified. In fact, it withstood practically every demolition strategy known to "future man," or at least men of 1967. Nothing was strong enough to defeat the almighty fortress that was the house of plastic—not chain saws, not fiery welding torches, not jack-hammers. Like a party guest overstaying its welcome, the house simply refused to leave. As Astro, the Jetson's talking dog, might have eloquently put it, "Ruh-roh."

Eventually, the house had to be divided before it could be conquered. It was sectioned off in pieces, each one sheared off individually by a scary piece of machinery called a "choker chain" (try asking for one at Lowe's and see what kind of looks you get) and disposed of bit by bit, *Rear Window* style. Actually, you *can* get choker chains, and they come equipped with steel probes (ouch), too. They're used to handle large logs. If *that* doesn't scare an inoffensive House of the Future just sitting there after proudly being viewed by twenty million guests, I don't know what would. The cement to which it clung with a barnacle's tenaciously can still be found, although it is now painted Disneyland's signature "go-away green," the color that fades into the background, and supports innocuous planters. House of Tomorrow, I will always miss you.

Not all futuristic attractions can claim such heroic status. Leisurely strolling through Tomorrowland these days, I can still envision the lengthy shadow cast by the TWA Rocket to the Moon. It looked like nothing so much as a red and white, pub-style, gigantic dart aimed straight at the sky. It was supported by several struts around the base holding it upright. This was an original attraction like the Mule Pack, one of those quintessential 1955 park landmarks. It lasted until 1975, a surprisingly long twenty-year run, when it was updated to become Mission to Mars. By then, few visitors even noticed or cared. Its time had long since come and gone, and so had the rocket. The rationale as to why anyone would "ride" this D-ticket attraction more than once is perplexing. Even as a very young guest, its appeal utterly eluded me.

A theatre full of us filed into a building and sat arrayed in concentric circles. There was no conceivable way for even a four year old like me to imagine that we had miraculously been crammed into the narrow, elongated rocket standing just outside, regardless of what the stentorian voice emanating from the "command center" claimed. Two small television-type screens, one high on the ceiling, the other on the floor, showed us where we were going on our voyage and where we had been.

10-9-8-7-6-5-4-3-2-1! Blast-off!

How did we know we were really blasting off? Because the speakers in the theatre made lots and lots of noise and our seats slowly moved perhaps an inch in a downward direction. They moved in the opposite direction upon re-entry.

You could see a tiny Disneyland, then Anaheim, then California, then the United States, and finally the planet itself disappearing beneath us on the floor screen as an increasingly larger moon loomed ahead of us on the ceiling screen. The images were black and white and somewhat fuzzy. A few "crew members" ordered us around officiously and issued stern warnings about the space-travel dangers we faced. They voiced tremendous relief as we safely touched back down once more in good old Anaheim.

Whew! That was a close one!

We obediently filed back out of the theatre as another group of space travelers filed in on our heels. Blinking outside in the bright California sunlight, we were back again on Mother Earth, *terra firma*. There stood the busy rocket poised for yet another lunar mission. The fact that it remained quite firmly bolted to the ground all day long undermined the illusion of flight so carefully cultivated by our intrepid flight crew. All systems might be *GO*, but the rocket never did.

Did Maleficent put a curse on Tomorrowland? The PeopleMover, an attraction we rode on our tours, Monsanto's ill-fated Journey Through Inner Space ("We're shrinking, *shrinking, SHRINKING...*"), the Skyway to Tomorrowland, and the Carousel of Progress (remember how well *that* went over on the VIP tour?) all eventually met the same fate as the Rocket to the Moon and the hapless House of Tomorrow, along with a myriad of other unlucky, unpopular venues "of the future." Space Mountain was the first attraction in quite some time to definitively succeed where so many others had failed. It was a palpable hit from its inception and continues to coast on a wave of tremendous popularity. It was built over the former employee parking lot and opened in 1977, five years after I led my last tour.

As much as any of the attractions of the past, I miss the wide expanse of the old parking lot. Disney's California Adventure currently sprawls across what was once the private playground and last frontier of the scrappy corps of parking lot attendants. The lot was larger than what you'd find inside the confines of the berm, about 100 acres to the park's 72 during my tour guide years. That adds up to more than the original purchase of 160 Anaheim acres, so either my math skills are more abysmal than I realized or a few additional acres were bought and utilized at some point.

Today, you'll find hugely imposing, impersonal multi-tiered parking structures adjacent to Disneyland with pre-recorded spiels spooling on the constantly running shuttles. New parking spaces have been added, but something much more has been lost. No more spontaneous, irreverent humor from the driver. No more ribald exchanges between the driver and the attendant who always rode along on the rear of the shuttle. No wild and crazy parking lot Olympics. No cozy golf-cart rides up and down every row in the pouring rain, accompanied by a solicitous parking lot attendant, searching for a car that stubbornly refuses to be found.

If you got to Disneyland early enough, right when it opened, you could simply park your vehicle, get out, and walk right up to the main gate. Simple as that. No need to even write down reminders on your parking stub to guide you back to said vehicle at the end of the day. There was an immediacy, an intimacy that has been irrevocably lost. It was possible to gauge the crowd you'd find inside by where you parked, too. Our hearts sank if we drove through the entrance to find the lot already mostly covered with cars. You could be stuck in the distant wastelands of Sleepy, Thumper, or Tinker Bell. Our hearts positively sang if we were waved to a parking slot up front like Bambi or Alice.

The fanciful, familiar welcome sign with its classic gothic script was playfully crowned with "waving" metal flags. It first appeared in 1958 and immediately achieved landmark status. The only other California sign as famous are those big white capital letters on a mountain over in Hollywood. I've no idea where the original parking lot sign is now, but John Stamos bought part of the one that welcomed park guests from 1989 to 1999 at auction for thirty grand and change.

That instantly recognizable Harbor Boulevard sign ushered in endless carloads of guests from every corner of the North American continent. We tour guides met our busloads of guests from around the world there. We walked past cars with license plates from widely scattered United and Mexican states and Canadian provinces while on the way to meet our buses. Alaska. Michoacán. Newfoundland. This was before air travel became commonplace. It was National Lampoon's *Vacation* personified, except that unlike Walley World, we were practically always open. There was no viable alternative, either—no Magic Mountain, no cluster of Walt Disney World theme parks in Florida, no Six Flags over Texas or anywhere else, no Universal Orlando. You wanna play the game? Well, we were the only game in town. If you want the kids to see Disneyland, pack 'em in the car with Grandma and gas 'er up—the car, not Grandma.

Like practically everything else, Disneyland changes. Some changes, like those from an earthquake, are instantaneous and cataclysmic. Others are incremental, well-planned, and carefully executed. Those at Disneyland can be wonderful and exciting like the additions of Indiana Jones, Big Thunder Mountain Railroad, Space Mountain, Haunted Mansion, Pirates, and *all* of New Orleans Square. They continue to breathe new life and vitality into the sixty-year-old park.

Others linger inexplicably. You wish in vain they would just go, already. Lookin' at you, Roger Rabbit. You, too, Toontown.

How could the walkthrough snore known as *20,000 Leagues Under the Sea* manage to hang around for eleven long years? Even after it was finally closed, it was never simply pitched. As was the case with my mother's garage, everything even remotely salvageable at Disneyland was stashed away. I suppose you just never know when a huge rubber squid might come in handy.

"Yeah, okay," you can almost hear someone in management propose with a sigh. "Let's just pass it on over to Disney Paris. After all, Jules Verne was French, wasn't he?"

Look for the town of Rainbow Ridge of Mule Pack fame next time you ride Thunder Mountain. The guiding mantra at Disneyland has always been "waste not, want not." You have only to witness the transmogrification of Bear Country into Critter Country. Did you honestly think we wouldn't notice?

Still other attractions seem practically doomed from their inception to quickly fade away. How many guests even recall, much less lament, the passing of the Aluminum Hall of Fame, the Viewliner, Dutch Boy Color Gallery, Crane Company Bathroom of Tomorrow, Holidayland, and Keller's Jungle Killers? Yes, you heard that last one right.

"*O tempora o mores,*" Cicero observed from the floor of the Roman Senate. Times and customs certainly do alter. Even though he rejected the label, Bob Dylan, the voice of my generation, noted the same irrefutable fact as he sang, "The times, they are a 'changin....'"

Attractions come and they go. Plants and trees continue to grow. Old familiar landmarks are leveled while others rise up to take their places. The Disneyland of memory, though, is always there for us who knew and loved it back when it was just getting started. To see it again, all you have to do is close your eyes, open your mind, and let your heart remember.

Our Daughter
Pilots a Submarine

"I'm gonna drive a sub," our daughter told us when she called from Anaheim.
"But girls don't do that," I told her.
"They do now!"

It was true. By the time Liz was ready to start training for her summer job at Disneyland, the entire park staff—excepting upper management, of course—had gone completely co-ed. This change had been instituted in 1995, forty years after opening day, and she would be working there during the summer of 1996. For anyone who has forgotten, women were only granted the right to vote in 1920, a year after my mother was born. The nineteenth amendment to the United States Constitution was passed on June 4, 1919, ratified on August 18, 1920. By the time American women could cast a ballot, formerly enslaved men had been voting for fifty years.

Our daughter would be among the pioneering cadre of young ladies implementing this momentous shift. It had been tried in 1974 and again in 1982 on the Jungle Cruise, according to Supervisor of Narration Attractions Bruce Kimbrell. He was interviewed by Marla Jo Fisher in an article she wrote for the *Orange County Register* on July 14, 1995. Unfortunately, Bruce told her, "guests didn't want to see women in those roles." The "puns didn't take." Helen Reddy might have had something interesting to say about that. In fact, you can almost hear her singing, "I am woman, hear me roar...."

Believe it or not, men had initially done the sweet little Storybook Land Canal spiels, but that role very quickly switched to women-only. In 1958, a couple of guys (Bill Skiles and Peter Henderson, Hub and Bub from *The Mickey Mouse Club* television show) who worked at the Plaza Gardens led guided tours; since the 1960s, tour guides had been exclusively female, while Jungle skippers, RETLAW employees, and *Mark Twain* and Submarine Voyage pilots were male. Men drove the Main Street vehicles, were sweepers, and loaded the gondolas of the Skyway between Tomorrowland and

Fantasyland. Then, forty years later, our daughter was hired just as Disneyland's strict gender roles were undergoing a sea change.

Lisa Barnaby, an employee at Disneyland, had visited Walt Disney World in Florida while on a vacation. (Yes, of course, Disney employees love Disney vacations, just like everyone else.) She saw female skippers on the Jungle Cruise and came back asking about it. Thanks to her timely inquiry and a more auspicious political climate, she was soon the first woman skipper on the Jungle Cruise in park history. She said that her guests certainly never seemed to mind. When asked about having a woman drive the boat, one girl noted, "At least if we get lost out there, she's a woman so she'll stop and ask for directions!"

Times change, and so does Disneyland, albeit sometimes more slowly than in the outside world. The first summer I worked at the park, Aunt Jemima's Pancake House, whose name was later changed to Aunt Jemima's Restaurant, was no more. Aunt Jemima herself, a popular character greeting guests since 1955, was out of luck, too. That character, a holdover from the old plantation days, no longer reflected the modern Disneyland image, and by 1970 the restaurant had become the River Belle Terrace. It was where the annual tour guide breakfast was held, and it was the first time I had ever been inside the restaurant. My family was never allowed the luxury of having breakfast at the park since it was only twenty minutes from home. The Yippies and any Black Panthers hoping to make a point searched for Aunt Jemima in vain that August in 1970.

It was in this brave new gender-free, race-conscious park that our nineteen-year-old daughter Liz found herself. By this time, we lived in Iowa City. She was out there completely on her own navigating the potentially treacherous waters of Anaheim, California. She had initially been assigned to work on Roger Rabbit's Car Toon Spin. Ho-hum. Like me, though, she didn't just accept what was being handed out. I can't stress enough the importance of letting people know what it is that you want. Don't be an observer in your own life. All anyone can tell you is "no."

"What else do you have?"

And that is how she ended up being trained and supervised as a submarine pilot by an ex-Navy SEAL. There were just four other young women who would be training along with her. What mother hasn't dreamed of the day her daughter says to her, "Mom, my submarine ran out of gas and had to be towed back to port."

That was actually one of the less significant of the mishaps possible on the subs. An oft-repeated story that sounds suspiciously more (sub) urban legend than fact is the time a submarine filled with close to forty Japanese citizens supposedly "sank" on December 7 in 1974. That seems like a curious amount of coincidence to me. The story goes that a trainer's ship rising to the dock hit it, and the crash popped out a couple of portholes. The water is only about four feet deep, so there was no serious danger. Had this actually happened, you'd think the incident would have received wider press coverage, wouldn't you? Sometimes, the boats actually do derail and drift helplessly until they can be towed to safety.

Subs were slow to load, a fatal flaw in the increasingly busy, fast-paced park. The gunmetal gray boats were named after the eight original nuclear-powered submarines in the US fleet. They had short, strong names like *Skate*, *Skipjack*, and *Seawolf*. You could almost hear a captain barking out those names as the subs took their passengers under the Arctic ice cap. Each one cost about $80,000. The track itself ran close to 1,400 feet. It was an exciting E-ticket ride, and the queue was almost always long. By the time our Liz became a pilot, they had been painted bright yellow and resembled research subs.

In the years 1965–1967, shortly before I worked at the park, live mermaids were a popular part of the attraction. They'd pose seductively on the coral reefs and wave at passing guests. Sometimes, they combed their long, beautiful hair. Disneyland is located close to a number of military bases. During my time at the University of Disneyland, we were told that a randy sailor on shore leave had actually jumped over the short fence and swam out to the mermaids who were no longer waving coyly by the time he got there, but were instead swimming as fast as their little fins allowed in the opposite direction. It has also been reported that the chlorine was too rough on their skin and hair, the diesel fumes too toxic. Personally, I prefer the amorous sailor story. Regardless of which is true, mermaids didn't last.

We guides sometimes spent as much as three-and-a-half solid hours of working with our guests on days when the park was exceptionally busy. No water breaks, no lunch breaks, no breaks of any kind. We walked, talked, and rode the rides right along with our people. Back to the lounge or the Pit, grab a quick lunch, and then head out with a second group. We earned our money and worked hard. By the end of the day, our dogs were barking.

When Liz became a member of the caste at Disneyland, the kids in the college program worked forty-five minutes on, fifteen off. It was like permanent area hostessing. I realize this sounds like your gramps telling you, "We knew what work was, by cracky! None of that new-fangled, sissy stuff called 'breaks' for us, no sir." Well, it might sound like Gramps talking, but it's true nonetheless. Liz and her future husband Amos worked forty-five minutes and then had a fifteen-minute break. That kind of schedule was reserved only for the likes of Mickey and company "back in my day." Okay, I feel like shaking my fist right now and saying something along the lines of "you kids keep off my lawn!"

I asked my son-in-law if he still remembered his Disneyland interview some twenty years after the fact.

"Of course," he said. "There were several of us in the room at the same time." That was different from my experience when I'd been the only one on the hot seat. "They asked the guy right before me to describe himself using three adjectives."

Most people know that question is coming in just about any interview now and are prepared. That poor guy didn't, though.

"Uh, um, uh...not really. I can't really think of any."

It's entirely possible that he simply didn't understand the meaning of the word "adjective". It's also possible he was frozen with a bad case of nerves. Next, the interviewer turned to Amos and asked him the same question.

"Sneezy, Happy, and Dopey," Amos said without batting an eye.

"You're *hired!*"

Maybe the tour guides were a bunch of goody-two-shoes, maybe supervisors were a little less scrupulous in 1996 than they were in 1969, and maybe both of those things were true. After hearing about some of the hijinks the operators pulled on Small World, it was a small miracle my future son-in-law actually made it all the way through to the end of summer.

The crew of wacky gondoliers would take turns hiding a small plastic turtle at various locations throughout the ride. Employees would determine how long it took to uncover the hiding place of the elusive amphibian. As often happens, what started as a little game among friends to alleviate the tedium quickly turned highly competitive.

"Last lily pad, rain forest—oh, yeah!"

"Taj Mahal behind middle dancer—nailed it!"

Amos assures me that he holds the reigning record for most successful secret turtle hiding place, and I urge you to check next time you ride. For all we know, it's still there.

"You know that guy with the flat hat that goes back and forth over the boats on a wire holding a balancing pole and riding a little cycle?" he once asked me.

"Yeah." I know everything on that ride.

"Top of his hat."

"How in the Small World did you get it up there?"

Amos told me, and then said, "And as far as I know, it was never found." He smiled like the Cheshire Cat.

For all *any* of us knows, a tiny plastic turtle was sentenced to an eternity of crossing and recrossing a wire on the hat of a cyclist. Makes the gig Sisyphus had look pretty appealing by comparison, doesn't it?

Believe me, there is nothing you could mention to me in that ride that would not be familiar. In fact, the conversations in the tour guide lounge often centered around which parts of which attractions were broken. It got so that was all we looked for after many hundreds trips through the same five attractions.

"Hyena isn't laughing."

"Skeleton isn't drinking."

"Cabin isn't burning."

"Pterodactyl isn't flapping," someone would say matter-of-factly in the same way someone else might observe, "Nice weather today." It was a kind of shorthand code for the fact that the wings of the ancient pterosaur, the one positioned next to the glass, were not currently in operation on the Primeval World section of the train ride.

In the same vein, there would sometimes be rather heated exchanges about the many cryptic song lyrics. Diamond was adamant about what the new-in-1972 County Bear Jamboree's largest ursine character was singing.

"No," she claimed with perfect certainty, "Big Al is saying: 'There was BUGS on the saddle and BUGS all around and a great big puddle of BUGS on the ground.'"

"Listen, Diamond, I know it sounds like he's saying *bugs*, but he isn't." I tried to be as patient as I could because, yes, it did sound like he was saying exactly that. "Think about it, though. How could there ever be a puddle of bugs? It doesn't make sense."

"Yeah, no way can it be bugs," Ruby added, coming to my defense.

"So if it isn't bugs, what is it, then?" Diamond's brown eyes snapped defiantly.

"Blood. He's singing about blood. There must have been a shooting. He's a *cowboy* bear." You have to keep in mind that this was in the days before such arguments could quickly be settled on a cell phone by accessing the internet, neither of which had been invented.

"Bugs," Diamond muttered darkly under her breath. "It's *bugs*."

Where else but in the Happiest Place on Earth could tour guides practically come to blows about song lyrics? Yet again, my sincere and heartfelt thanks go to you, Johnny Depp, for clearing up, once and for all, that jolly-fried-eggs conundrum on Pirates.

The point is, riding the same things over and over again causes you to focus on the oddest details. Lyrics, broken audio-animatronic figures, even the placement of a tiny turtle, all take on inordinately large importance. You *had* to focus on something or you'd go crazy. It made Bill Murray's *Groundhog Day* experience look like amateur hour. Different operators on the various attractions had different ways to banish boredom.

Once, while a supervisor was briefly out of the picture, Amos and a cohort decided to see what would happen if they let the guests load themselves in the Small World boats. Generally, you walk up to the operator loading an attraction and tell that person how many people you have in your party. If it's noisy, I just hold up my fingers like a three year old. Then, the operator will tell you to take row one or rows three and four—whichever lines best accommodate the number of people in your particular group.

Amos decided to perform some impromptu market research to see what would happen if he and a friend allowed people to load themselves into the boat. I don't know of many people who would think of this, let alone actually do it.

"Where do we go?" asked the first confused guest. People were always told which row to use, and he had obviously been used to that protocol all day long at the park.

"Take whatever seat you like, sir." Amos swept his arm grandly toward the empty boat. His partner in crime smiled and nodded.

The man happened to be just the first of an extremely large group.

"C'mon everybody!" the man called enthusiastically to the remainder of his party.

They came and keep right on coming. Occasionally, one of them might look over quizzically at Amos and his gondolier partner for confirmation.

"It's okay. Load yourselves."

Kids sat on laps. The rows were hip to hip with hefty adults. Chug, chug, chug went the jam-packed boat, a little slower than usual, up the short conveyer ramp that leads the filled boats up to the canal before they float gently off it and settle into the slowly moving water. This time, however, instead of easing gently into the canal, the boat didn't budge once it left the ramp. It slowly sank beneath the ridiculously overloaded amount of weight it carried in full view of the waiting queue of horrified guests ready to board.

The water is shallow, no one was hurt, but one extremely large party of guests were wet to the knees that afternoon. Small children were passed from one adult to the next, save-my-baby fashion, until all were again safe on dry land. By this time, Amos and his bud, of course, were nowhere to be found. The guys were, no doubt, on their fifteen-minute break.

It's not as though a Small World boat mishap is unheard of, even under normal circumstances. My friend Chris told me about the time her father, Ruben, was unceremoniously dumped out of a Small World boat while waiting to disembark. I can easily understand how that could happen. On a busy day, boats pile up a bit. They push hard against each other like, well, like those unruly pack mules of yore. I had seen the sterns of boats rise majestically, tragically from the water, *Titanic*-like, on occasion myself. Ruben had simply stepped from the steeply tilted boat into the water and waded to shore. I only hope he was wearing shorts at the time.

By the time Liz and Amos worked at the park, Date Nite was a thing of the past. They might receive a few free passes at the end of the summer season, but no more of those Friday night freebies Ron and I enjoyed so much. They made close friends who are still in touch with each other twenty years later. At their wedding in 2006, the Disneyland College Program gang of six was reunited: Liz and Amos, of course, and also Jan (he's Norwegian and it's pronounced Yawn), Julie, Ryanna, and Michael. As the saying frequently repeated among employees goes, marriages are made in Disneyland, and this one reunited the group.

At the end of their summer as part-time cast members, Liz went back to the University of Iowa and Amos returned to UC Berkeley. Their romance, kindled in the park, continued to grow. They both ended up in graduate programs in LA, Amos at USC's Marshall School of Business MBA program, Liz at USC's Gould School of Law. After they were married, a Disney trip became their favorite family vacation. Their two children and I heartily agree—there's really nothing better.

Liz's Disney career included a part two. Following her summer in Anaheim, she worked the next summer in Orlando, making her a member of the elite group of bi-coastal Disney employees who worked in both magic kingdoms. Gender roles were not as entrenched there as they had been at Disneyland, probably due in large part to its later opening date. She worked on the Skyway, wore adorable lederhosen, and found out that while "it never rains in southern California," it rains practically every day in Orlando.

My father from Boston used to talk about "muggy" summers on the North Shore. Humidity in dry LA was a foreign concept, though, until I visited Acapulco in high school on a Spanish language trip. Walking outside the hotel room felt exactly like stepping into a warm shower. I had forgotten that uncomfortable sensation until we visited Liz in Florida. Walt Disney World sold "misters," little plastic fans attached to water bottles that sprayed you to try to keep you cooler. There were also giant mist fans set up to blow on the long summer lines of people, aka, queues of guests. It was so uncomfortable that it practically took your breath away. Small wonder we got a surprisingly good deal on our Sanibel Island digs! No one goes there in the summer if they can avoid it. I highly recommend visiting in January. It's perfect then.

On the WDW Skyway, there was the Disney version of the "mile high club," created by those amorous, flexible couples who had managed to use the rocking gondola as their private trysting place. There was the frequent smell of marijuana smoke as kids so inclined managed to sneak a joint on the trip between lands. What finally closed the Skyway for good, though, was not people and their peccadilloes. It was the fatal combination of the ride being slow to load, and sometimes forced to a complete stop when understandably timid guests were reluctant to fling caution to the winds and jump into a moving aeriel gondola, and the presence of Florida's frequent afternoon storms. Flashes of lightning, crashing booms of thunder, and the drenching rains never lasted very long, but they lasted long enough to shut down the Skyway once too often. It was finally closed for good.

When she returned to college that fall, Liz became the University of Iowa campus representative for Walt Disney World's College Program. She told other university students about the benefits of working seasonally at the Magic Kingdom. Some company lines were empty, some had just a few college kids waiting in them, but Liz's line was always long and winding. Not only that, the faces she met were smiling. The prospect of working at a place like Walt Disney World was every bit as exciting for these Midwestern kids as working at Disneyland had been for me.

The training you receive at the University of Disneyland (now Disney University) will last a lifetime. Interacting with guests from countries around the world provides experiences you simply could never have working anywhere else. Making dreams come true is a job unlike any other you'll ever know. My "wish upon a star" is that some day, I'll get to see my own grandchildren working at Disneyland. It is a life-changing experience, one I wouldn't have missed for the world. If their parents hadn't met while working at Disneyland, they wouldn't be here today.

Someday I might even be fortunate enough to hear my delightful grand-daughter call me to say, "Grammy, I've been accepted into the Management Training Program at Disney!"

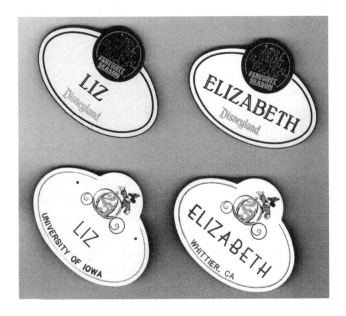

Sweets for the Suite

"Is this your tenth cruise with us?" the man asked, perfunctorily checking us in without making eye contact. No welcoming smile. Two groups were checking in, and there were two check-in desks with one person working at each. This guy needed a swift refresher course at Disney University.

"No. This is our first cruise with you," I told him. I didn't mention that it was our first cruise period, but it was.

"Oh." Still no smile.

The big, boisterous group of couples standing next to us all wore matching pastel T-shirts with the dates and destinations of their previous ten cruises with the Disney Cruise Line. They were checking into the Roy O. Disney Suite. I had booked the Walter E. Disney Suite many months before. A lot of people who stay in the fanciest suites on the ship do so because those suites were being given as an upgrade for their loyalty. Not us. We were paying for the privilege.

I retired from teaching the previous June, and now we were going to celebrate in style, Disney style. We would be going first class, living the suite life. *Whoo-hoo*. Joining me on the cruise were my daughter and her husband, also Disney alums, and their two children, ages three and six, *future* Disney alums. Once I saw the lavish interior of the suite on Disney's website, I couldn't look at anything else. It was absolutely perfect! The *Magic*, the first ship in the Disney fleet, was launched in 1998. It had just been completely refurbished, so we'd be the first guests to enjoy its brand-new décor.

There were two major benefits I saw for bumping up to the Walt Disney Suite: the incredible accommodations themselves and the two concierges who would be there to help us have a wonderful time on the trip. We decided to "bookend" the cruise, so we had just come from a stay at the fabulous Kidani Village, a Disney Vacation Club property, and several days visiting Disney's Animal Kingdom. A Disney-owned bus transported us to and from the port. Disney videos were shown, and we looked through porthole-shaped windows at the passing Florida landscape.

After the Bahamian cruise and a stop on our last day at sea at Castaway Cay, Disney's privately owned island, we would be transported back to the Magic Kingdom and stay at the Bay Lake Towers, another DVC property, while we visited the rest of the parks. We weren't members, but if you make reservations early enough, you can get the very same rooms as the members do, and the suites are great. Where else can you cook breakfast in your own fully-equipped kitchen in the morning, walk directly into the Magic Kingdom in less than ten minutes, and watch fireworks in pajamas on your private balcony at night?

Our trip was in early January, right at the start of the bitter Midwest winter. The lavish, gorgeous holiday decorations at Disney World were still very much in place. It was as fabulously festive as only Disney does it and made the holidays that year feel like they just kept going and going and going....

Living on the Left Coast, Ron and I always hoped to take a cruise to Alaska. We never managed to make it happen, but we had spent quite a bit of time looking longingly at ships and shipboard rooms. The vast majority of them seemed so claustrophobic, so downright dinky. We definitely didn't want to be housed in the modern equivalent of steerage. My McGann ancestors from County Longford, Ireland, had already been there, done that, on the three-masted schooner *Neptune* in 1866. Nope, not this time. This was going to be a once-in-a-lifetime trip. We'd pull out all the stops.

My language arts classes studied the voyage of the *Titanic* for years—even before James Cameron decided to make his Academy-Award-winning film. I'd been interested in the subject ever since reading Walter Lord's *A Night to Remember* in sixth grade, and that interest had revived after Robert Ballard located the wreck in 1985. A colleague told me how he would allow his sixth graders to work collaboratively constructing a model on Friday afternoons, as long as they were caught up on their work. What a good idea! I bought my class a model of the *Titanic* and things snowballed.

Some of the students were absolutely convinced Mr. Cameron had heard about and been inspired by our amazing, original plays on the subject. Our productions were as elaborate, realistic, and well-researched as we could possibly make them. Once, there was even a fishing boat with oars hauled onstage for the survivors following the ill-fated collision with the iceberg.

Sometimes, there were flubs of lines during rehearsal like this one delivered earnestly by one of my favorite boys: "How are we supposed to spot binoculars without any icebergs?"

I would give what I thought was a very credible demonstration of a British accent to inspire the young actors getting into character.

"Mrs. Keech, you sound like an Australian. In fact, you sound like the Crocodile Hunter."

For the remainder of that year, every once in a while, someone would pop up with a clever line like, "Crikey, there's a croc on the 'berg, and she's a beauty," always said in an Australian accent so thick you could cut it with a knife.

One year, I thought I'd finally be vindicated when a nice young man from London joined our class.

"Edward, tell me the truth. Don't you think this is a pretty good British accent?"

I gave it a go with something silly and off-the-cuff. "Let's throw some jelly babies at the Beatles. I just adore the lads from Liverpool."

He was so tactful. "It actually sounds a bit more Australian than British."

Crikey, mate. I give up.

There were always adorable girls portraying the snooty first-class passengers who had the world at their feet. The spunkiest of them played Molly Brown. Grandmothers' furs came out of mothballs. Long, satin evening gloves to their elbows, feathers in their hats, tiny stuffed toy dogs on their laps, and lots of attitude were all displayed in abundance. Nineteen twelve was the gilded age, a time when luxury on a grand scale unimaginable today was a matter of course on the ship nicknamed "The Millionaire's Special." After many years of study, I did know something about first class. I couldn't wait to experience just one small taste of that rarified world.

We followed directions delivered cheerfully from a nautical greeter in the ship's lobby and found our way up to the eighth floor, starboard side. Our rooms were located in the middle of the corridor, the most stable part of the ship. There was a doorbell outside Suite 8030—a doorbell that the children of guests staying nearby would soon gleefully ring as they played ding-dong-ditch. Walking inside the front door was like going back in time. Light wood paneling, the kind my parents' generation called "blond," and a series of gracefully curved built-ins were taken straight from the 1930s when Walt was making his mark in Hollywood.

Personal photos of the Disney family and Walt riding the *Lilly Belle* in his Holmby Hills backyard, books about his railroading hobby, fresh flowers, and Disney memorabilia were on prominent display. With some rooms on some ships, it's pretty cool to get an outside balcony. The balcony of this suite ran the length of four huge rooms giving us an unobstructed view of the roiling ocean far below. Bathrooms are often tiny and multipurpose on cruise lines. The master bedroom had its own jetted soaker tub and separate shower. The rounded Deco counters were fashioned from black marble. Adjacent to it was an expansive book-lined study with more beautiful built-ins and a desk overlooking the water. By the time we had explored the rooms, we were practically giddy. Could this really all be ours?

"Grammy, are we going to live here now?" my three-year-old grandson asked, wide-eyed.

"No, honey, we're just visiting." And please, *please* don't break anything!

A dining room for eight! An enormous couch and chairs on peacock-feather patterned carpet in the living room! A complete bar area with all kinds of waiting welcome fruit and snacks! Bunk beds for the little ones with their own large bathroom! Closets to hold Louis Vuitton-sized steamer trunks full of clothes with no problem (no, we didn't actually *have* those; I'm just saying they *could* have fit if we did). Another bathroom? That makes *three!* The place seemed to go on forever. It was considerably bigger than most apartments and condos we had lived in when Ron and I were younger, and the finishes and furnishings were breathtakingly opulent. It felt almost like a maiden voyage because everything was new. Oh, wait. Too reminiscent of the *Titanic.* Better not to think about that right now.

"Attention all passengers. Attention all passengers. Report immediately to your assigned lifeboat loading area for the lifeboat drill." The voice over the intercom was stern and serious. No more "have a magical day."

After the *Titanic* sank, maritime law was forever changed. Now, every ship must hold a lifeboat drill, something tragically dispensed with on the very day the great ship had sunk. The so-called "unsinkable ship" had been as long as three football fields, 882.5 feet. It was the largest moving, man-made object on earth. The *Magic* was even larger at 965 feet. There must now be a seat on a lifeboat assigned for every passenger and crew member. The *Titanic* had barely half that number, and some of those boats were sent off nearly empty before the gravity of the situation was fully understood. By then, of course, it was too late.

Dutifully, guests filed up to the top deck joining streams of passengers from various lower decks. We easily found our assigned lifeboat. Everything was smooth and orderly. I couldn't help envisioning the scene of panic on the night of April 14, 1912. Looking over the sides of the railing into the dark gray ocean churning far below, it was hard not to shiver remembering the many unfortunate people lost. There were life vests for us all. This was the serious part of the voyage. It didn't last very long.

Next stop? Cocktail party with Donald Duck!

We already knew our rooms were sw-*eeeet!* Now we would meet our two concierges, have some (more) fancy snacks and drinks, and the little ones would have some two-on-one time with Donald Duck, who came in wearing a tuxedo—or at least the top half of a tuxedo. As usual, the devil-may-care little duck wore no pants.

The lounge was swanky-cool with a 1930s jazz club theme in tones of silver, black, and blue. Only folks who sprung for or were bumped up to a suite were invited to this exclusive little get-acquainted soirée; the setting was intimate, the mood excited. We sat sipping and munching by gigantic portholes as the sun went down. A person could get used to this!

Working their way around the small room were the friendly concierges. I couldn't begin to imagine the wild things they had seen and done, the unusual demands they had tried to meet, the strange orders they had done their best to follow. These were the true pros of the hospitality world. They worked at the pinnacle of guest relations on the ship. As soon as they sat down beside us to introduce themselves, it was clear we were in good hands.

"Welcome, welcome! Anything you need, anything you want, please do not hesitate to let us know. Reservations to anything on the ship or on shore, we will take care of it all for you," the man assured us.

"Call on us at any time. We are so happy to have you with us. Have you traveled with us before?" the woman asked.

Two pairs of dark brown eyes sparkled as they greeted us with genuine pleasure. This was the warm welcome we had missed at check-in. Yes, it's a job. I am well aware this isn't a volunteer position. Neither was being a tour guide, but if it's a job you enjoy, you take pride in doing it well. You really do have fun with your guests. It *is* a pleasure. We spent a few minutes sharing our cruise plans, some of the things we hoped to see and do while we were here.

After a while I told them, "We have all three worked at Disneyland, and my daughter also worked a summer at Walt Disney World."

"You *have*? Then you understand!" If his smile had been wide before, it practically glowed now.

"How wonderful! You understand," she echoed happily.

"Yes," I replied, mirroring their grins. "We certainly do."

This must be how strangers in a strange land feel when they encounter a countryman. There is a shared language, a shared culture, shared experiences. They all but threw their arms around our necks in recognition. Before, they had been poised, polished, and professional. Now, they both took a breath, relaxed, and settled back to chat with us like old friends.

They wanted to hear all about what we had done, how long we had done it, what years we had worked, and how we ended up on the *Magic* in the Walter E. Disney suite. This phenomena should be called the Brotherhood of Walt. Like the lyrics say in the "Brotherhood of Man", "we're dedicated to giving all we can." It really is "a noble tie that binds." Employees, whenever and whenever they meet, immediately understand and appreciate each other's unique training and common background. It's a shorthand way of saying, "Yes, we get it."

That's just how I felt when I discovered one of the erudite, literate moms in my book club, now a teacher, worked in her previous life in Orlando as Chip and/or Dale and a couple of the dwarfs! Our connection was immediate. Oh, and she'd like me to please pass the word along to those enormous tour groups of beautiful Brazilian kids who visit the Magic Kingdom: Please don't hug the little chipmunks so *very* hard!

The two concierges were as good as their word. No matter what we needed, they made it happen. Book a dinner reservation, locate those luxurious terry robes like the ones in our suite to purchase and take home, reserve a casita for us on Castaway Cay? Sure, no problem. Having extremely competent helpers made the trip a relaxing joy, not a stress-filled scramble.

One afternoon, he showed up at our door with popcorn and DVD movies for the kids. Another day, she would come by with a plate of fancy goodies, just for fun.

"Would you like to have some chocolate strawberries?"

Well, what would *you* have said? Yeah, that's what I thought.

Every day brought another special treat, always delivered with smiles, good wishes, and inquiries as to our enjoyment of the ship and all it had to offer—and believe me when I say it had a lot to offer! Recommendations? They would gladly provide them. Clarification of policies and protocol? Definitely. Room service? Certainly. What about room service from Palo, the most exclusive restaurant on the ship? Of course! There really was nothing these two could not produce with a wave of their very helpful hands.

"Just call me Thurston Howell III," Amos said one morning, sounding as much like actor Jim Backus as humanly possible while sitting on the runway of a balcony outside our rooms leaning back in a lounge, cut crystal flute of still water raised in his hand. He was working on a laptop, wrapped in one of those luxurious terry robes, a pair of complimentary matching slippers with the Mickey cruise logo on his feet, and his three-year-old son's Mickey Mouse yachting cap set at a jaunty angle on his head. Every time I look at the photo I took of him, it makes me smile. It was ludicrous how easily we slipped on the mantle of the leisure class.

I don't see how even the famous grand staircase on the *Titanic* could have compared with the gleaming gold and silver accents, polished wood, intricately detailed, sea-themed, tiled mosaics, and sparkling crystal chandeliers of the ship's common spaces. Everywhere you looked, Mickey and Minnie, the Peter Pan crew, the Princesses, Goofy, and Donald and Daisy were there to dispense hugs and pose with everyone. They might be pirates one day, sailors the next. It was like living in a beautiful kaleidoscope.

Want some time for adult relaxation? There was a sitter service in the nursery area equipped with larger-than-life toys from *Toy Story* in a fantasy playground setting. They looked liked they might have been movie props, and knowing the Disney company, that's entirely possible. There were camps of all kinds for our six year old like cooking, science, drama, and games. Once, Stitch came running through the campers shooting a squirt gun and convulsing them with his alien antics. In fact, there were activities especially designed for children of all ages and interests. A movie theatre played current big-screen hits, so we could see *Saving Mr. Banks* knowing both the little ones were safe and happy for a couple of hours. Since my bedtime is about the same as the children, Liz and Amos could go out in the evenings to enjoy some *Magic* night life, secure in the knowledge that three-fifths of the party were safely tucked in for the night, while visions of chocolate strawberries danced in their heads.

Then, it was time for a day on Castaway Cay. Of the thousand or so acres, only about fifty-five are developed. Some Disney employees actually live there. It's a lovely little gem in the ocean.

I like the island's former name, Gorda Cay. It means Fat Cay, a prosaic image Disney quickly changed. The name was originally given because of the hump-shaped nature of the terrain. Castaway, however, must have sounded better than Hunchback of Notre Dame Cay around the brainstorming tables.

"Hey, we've still got some of that stuff left over from *20,000 Leagues Under the Sea*," a bright junior manager might have said at some point in the Castaway Cay development meeting. "Disney Paris didn't even want it."

"Seriously? I thought they'd take anything, especially anything with Jules Verne's name on it. So what, exactly, are you proposing we do with it," a senior manager might have asked.

"Let's just dump it offshore on Castaway Cay! Snorkelers can see it. Fish will swim around it. It costs practically nothing beyond the cost to transport it. It can't miss!"

"Brilliant, Jason! I *like* it!"

Ah, *20,000 leagues Under the Sea*, the gift that keeps on giving. Think of that when you see the submerged wreck of the submarine *Nautilus* next time you're snorkeling off Castaway Cay.

It is said that pirates may have used the island. A large ingot of silver and some coins were found off the shore by treasure seekers decades ago. They are thought to be from the *San Pedro*, a Spanish galleon that sank in 1733 on its way back to fill the coffers of King Philip IV. The pirate possibility is far enough removed from present times to be interesting and romantic in a yo-ho-ho sort of way. Actual pirates aren't nearly so much fun, but movie pirates are delightful. After filming wrapped on *Pirates of the Caribbean*, Captain Jack Sparrow's *Black Pearl* graced the bay on Castaway Cay for a while. Somewhere buried deep in the Disney Archives must be the prime directive: Reuse movie props whenever, wherever, and however possible.

The island had another image problem, this one more recent and well-documented. Before Disney purchased it, this busy little cay did a booming business in the drug-trafficking trade. The airstrip from its time spent as Drug Smuggling Cay is still there and connects a couple of the island's beaches to each other. People riding bikes on the runway today ride in the shadows of those drug lords and their armed enforcers. Now, the island is clean, shiny, and as close to a tropical paradise as you can imagine.

We boarded the little trolley from the ship and rode it around to the opposite side of the bay. There were many small buildings scattered loosely around a central cluster. Wandering past the shops with palm-frond covered roofs, rest rooms, and places to eat, we finally came to the entrance leading to the long, arcing row of casitas along the shoreline. Is it a splurge to rent one? Yes. Should you do it anyway? Also, yes. Don't get one of the high numbers like #27 because the rest rooms are located next to #1, and those are the *only* rest rooms.

"Look, they know our name!" My granddaughter was surprised, pointing. "But how did they know we were coming?"

Oh, honey, they know *everything*.

A charming, rustic sign outside Casita #3 greeted us by name. Who doesn't want their own little beach house nestled among the palms on the baby-blue Caribbean? We couldn't actually buy one, of course, but we could certainly settle in for one very indulgent day. A front deck with lounges and tables, an interior with coastal-patterned chairs and couches, a kitchen area with stocked mini-fridge, as many extra towels as any four families could possibly use—this pretty, pastel place had it all.

Just off the deck, there were a couple of commodious rope hammocks on the little sandy path leading down to the shore where the kids immediately set about collecting shells and splashing in the waves. Across the bay, the *Magic* was docked, our temporary home away from home. It was the final day, and we were definitely still livin' the good life.

Jet skis, petting gooshy rays (not their scientific name, no, but the adjective my granddaughter used to describe their jello-soft heads), riding bikes, a barbecue, Bahama-style hair wraps—and how did the skilled beautician with her flying fingers manage to braid and wrap my granddaughter's hair with colorful embroidery threads so much faster than I could unwrap it two weeks later? There was a lot on offer to keep pampered guests hopping. You could do as much or as little as you wanted. The memories we made on the trip will last us a lifetime.

Our concierge hurried by on the path as we headed to lunch. She was dressed in a bright, flowing, flowered-print gown and looked the very picture of island royalty. As soon as she recognized us, she stopped to say hello.

"They have you doing something different today, don't they?" I asked her, nodding at her pretty costume.

"Of course," she laughed ruefully. "*You* know how it works."

Yes, I sure did, except for me, the "something else" had been Disneyland Information, the Magic Kingdom Club, or area hostessing. Chalk another one up to the Brotherhood of Walt.

As incredible as it all was, could you live the suite life every day?

"Too much hot fudge sundae," my aunt used to say. What she meant was, you'd soon get sick of over-indulging in anything that was too rich.

Well, we wouldn't have to find out if that old saying were true or not because this first-class experience wasn't something we'd be able to repeat any time soon. Even so, it was one that truly had made our dreams come true. The only bittersweet part was that Ron wasn't there to enjoy it with us. He would have loved every single minute.

All good things must come to an end, and our trip finally did. We had just sat down to a spectacular dinner at the Artist's Palette. It was the last night of the cruise, and our waiter, who rotated through the restaurants right along with us, knew what we liked, or, in case of our little ones, didn't like.

"Water, no ice, right, sir?" The charming waiter smiled and set the glass down in front of my grandson with a flourish.

Who were we dining with, James Bond Jr.? If you think it isn't a slippery slope getting spoiled rotten, think again.

"Mac and cheese for the little princess." Another dazzling smile for my granddaughter.

I was glad that both of them had been raised to be polite and appreciative because they immediately said "thank you" with no parental (or grandparental) prompting.

Soft lights of fuchsia, aqua, lemon, and lime lit up the room. The Disney characters appeared, dancing among the diners, much to everyone's delight. We watched, as our courses were brought to the table, the enormous black-and-white sketches on the walls surrounding us slowly transformed into the colorful, familiar images from Disney films. It was a celebration, an homage to the art of animation. Giant paintbrushes decorated the entire scene.

When it was over, we joined the other guests for a live show in the ship's giant, plush theater. I can't imagine *Peter Pan* done better, even on Broadway. It was like seeing the old story unfold right before our eyes complete with pixie dust, the Darling kids taking flight for the first time, and Neverland made real. Even better than seeing it ourselves was watching it through the eyes of the two sweet children with us. These two über-modern, plugged-in, iPad kids who could hardly hold still at times sat rapt, entirely enthralled with the action unfolding onstage.

We had sailed the Caribbean on a magnificent ship, felt like honored guests of Walt himself in our luxury suite, spent time in our fabulous island casita right on the beach, had the two best concierges in the fleet helping grant our every wish like a pair of benevolent fairy godparents, were on a first-name basis with the whole cavalcade of Disney characters on board, and had been transported for just a little while into a rarified world we had only imagined.

Life doesn't get much sweeter than spending time having fun together with all three generations of the family. That was the whole idea behind the creation of Disneyland. Walt imagined a place where he could have fun *with* his daughters, where adults could do more than just sit on a bench and watch. His legacy continues to grow, and from the iconic films, to Disneyland, to Walt Disney World, to the Disney Cruise Line, we've grown up right along with it. Our brief taste of "the suite life" turned out exactly right. Sometimes, if you're very lucky, dreams really do come true.

And speaking of making dreams come true, the next time you visit Disneyland, my favorite park, check out the dancing scene in the Haunted Mansion, the one where the men in the paintings come to life, turn, and fire at each other in a duel. See that gorgeous brass organ against the wall, the one with those ghostly skull musical notes pouring out of it? Where do you think the Imagineers found that spectacular, well-traveled musical instrument? If you've been paying attention, you won't have to guess, you'll know. There must have been a brainstorming meeting back in 1967.

"Boys, we're just about ready to break for lunch. Now, final item on the agenda. Can anyone think of someplace to stick that white elephant left over from *20,000 Leagues Under the Sea*? Anyone? C'mon now, or one of you is gonna be lugging it home."

The phalanx of junior executives seated around the polished conference table all looked blankly at each other and then uneasily back toward their boss. He wasn't known for being patient at the best of times, and at this point he was tired and getting hungry.

Finally, the sharpest among them, a real go-getter, snapped his fingers and rose.

"Hey, wait a minute! I've *got* it!" The rest listened hopefully. "Why don't we just drag it over to New Orleans Square and put it in that big ballroom scene in the Haunted Mansion. It'll fit right in!"

A hush fell over the conference room.

"Inspired, Jason. I *like* it!"

In school, we learned about the resourceful indigenous people of the great American plains who used every last part of the noble buffalo. Nothing went to waste. Meat, hide, sinews, hooves—a use was found for everything, regardless of how humble, and so it was with the resourceful executives at Disney.

That's right. The ghostly organ sitting in the ballroom of Disneyland's Haunted Mansion for nearly fifty years is the prop last played by the demented Captain Nemo aboard the *Nautilus* in *20,000 Leagues Under the Sea*.

Epilogue:
Once a Tour Guide,
Always a Tour Guide

Once you've worked at Disneyland, that little sparkle of pixie dust is always with you.

The other day, I was waiting to pick up my grandson at his preschool. One of the fathers walked right past the patiently waiting people in line, mostly young moms with babies in strollers or toddlers balanced on their hips. There are always some grandparents like me waiting there, too.

He acted as if we were invisible, just as he always does, and walked into the classroom, a breach of preschool protocol. We are supposed to wait in an orderly line until a teacher opens the door. Then the children are called, one at a time, to join their grown-up. I'm always dumbfounded at his boorish behavior, but after working at the park, it's especially galling to stand there as if nothing unusual is happening. Is it fun to wait your turn in line? Not especially. Do we do it anyway? Yes, because that's the way civilization works. You don't cut in front of people because you don't want to wait your turn.

Countless times, I've stood on blistering hot pavement with my twenty-plus guests packed closely together in a forty-five minute line. The mercury registers one hundred degrees, the southern California sun mercilessly beats down on us, as we wait to board a sixteen-minute attraction. Had someone attempted to cut in front of us, you can be sure there would have been a collective howl of protest if not downright anarchy.

Finally, exasperated, I asked of no one in particular, "Am I the only one who notices this? That guy always cuts the line. Does it bother anyone else?"

There were lots of nods, a couple of sheepish smiles of acknowledgement, and a few murmurs of assent.

"Well, I worked at Disneyland, and when people cut in line like that, it still drives me crazy!"

Quickly switching focus away from the actions of an ill-mannered father, the conversation immediately turned happy and animated with lots of smiles and sparkling eyes.

"You worked at Disneyland?"

"I did, yes."

"What did you do there?"

"I was a tour guide."

"Was it fun?"

"It was!"

"How long did you work there?"

"All through college during vacations."

"I wish I could have done that."

Of course you do. Everyone does. You can see the familiar, dreamy looks, the sparkling eyes, the wistful smiles as they imagine what it must be like to be a part of the Disney magic. I'd seen it on generations of my students' faces over the decades.

It's always like that, no matter how many years go by. People love hearing about my job at Disneyland. Yes, it really was every bit as cool as you might imagine—and then some! It's a learning experience like no other. Not only that, it's tremendously exciting and fun. From my point of view, there's no better preparation for getting along in life: be polite, wait your turn, be respectful of others. It's an experience I wouldn't trade for the world.

And boy, what I wouldn't have given just then for my trusty riding crop. I'd have snapped it sharply above my head and warned the errant dad, "Excuse me, sir, but *no* one is allowed to cut the line!"

You can take the tour guide out of Disneyland, but you can't take that Disneyland pixie dust out of the tour guide, and for that, I will always be grateful.

Acknowledgments

Thanks to everyone who read this manuscript and offered helpful suggestions and encouragement. Any mistakes remaining are, of course, my own. Other than the few individuals identified by name, characters are fictional creations based upon combinations of the traits of various people I knew while working at Disneyland. It's impossible to recall, verbatim, conversations that occurred decades ago, but in all cases I did my best to reconstruct the speakers' words and their intent as closely as possible. In a few cases, the fancifully imagined business meetings of Disney management, for example, were included strictly for purposes of humor and hyperbole. The actual events described in these pages, however, all happened to me.

Sincere appreciation goes especially to Amos, my wonderful son-in-law, for his expertise in all things Disney, his hilarious sense of humor, and for being such a great dad to my grandchildren, Katherine and Drew, and a terrific husband to my daughter, Liz.

Very special thanks also to Catherine, my lovely daughter-in-law, French teacher extraordinaire, and gourmet cook, who has not yet been to Disneyland but says my book made her want to go, and who is having my third grandchild very soon. Thank you, Cat, for finding my son, Rob, and making him so happy.

I appreciate more than words can say the kind, consistent input throughout the writing process from my dear friend, Anne. She was always eager to read the next chapter, even before it had been written. When I was discouraged, Anne always gave me just the right kind of enthusiastic feedback that I needed to continue. Her love of Disneyland touches my heart.

My long-time friend Linda remained convinced for many years that I played Snow White at Disneyland, no matter how often I denied it. Her daughter, Kristen, sang six shows a day at Mickey's Birthday Party at Walt Disney World before heading off to a successful Broadway career. My lucky day was the one Linda, my unofficial "big sister," moved in next door to us.

Thanks go to my marvelous friend Meg for being a hilarious and inspirational teaching partner for twelve happy years at Northwest. We loved teaching about literature and writing and were always in awe of the formidable talents shown by our students. I miss our Secret Passage, Joe Hardy, and I always will.

Without the gentle nudges and sometimes firmer shoves administered by my lovely and literate book club friends, I wouldn't read nearly as widely as I do, nor would I have believed I could tell an interesting story other people might actually want to read. Wendy, Margaret, Jane, Becky, and Sheral, thank you so much, ladies, for your unflagging support and encouragement.

Thanks to Zach, Gordon, and Joey, three of the most intelligent, kind, and amazing young men it has ever been my pleasure to teach, for consistently challenging me to become a better educator and person. Zach published his touching memoir, *My Two Moms*, before he was twenty-one, Gordon is a graduate of Amherst College and Harvard Law School, and Joey will be heading off to college this fall. All three are Eagle Scouts, and I was honored to write their recommendation letters for them.

Without having first read Annie Salisbury's highly engaging memoir *The Ride Delegate* (Theme Park Press, 2015) about her incredible VIP hostess experiences at Walt Disney World, I would have never even thought to write and share my Disneyland memories with you. Cheers, Annie!

Finally, I am forever indebted and tremendously grateful to Bob McLain, owner of Theme Park Press, for giving me this opportunity to share these tour guide tales with you.

And now, I'm going to Disneyland!

About the Author

Andrea McGann Keech was born in southern California and visited Disneyland often, ever since it opened in 1955. She fulfilled a life-long dream of working at the park and became a bilingual tour guide and VIP hostess during college holidays from 1969 through 1972.

She and husband Ron met at Occidental College in 1969 and were married in San Francisco in 1970. Ron graduated from the University of California at San Francisco Medical School, and Andrea finished college at the University of San Francisco. They lived in Portland, Oregon, for six years and then moved to Iowa City where he was a professor of medicine and a surgeon in the Department of Ophthalmology at the University of Iowa for twenty-two years until his death in 2007. Their children, Elizabeth and Robert, made them incredibly proud and very happy parents. Liz is an attorney, and Rob is a dentist.

Andrea taught students in English and Spanish in grades K-12 during her teaching career. She was a member of the National Assessment of Educational Progress Committee, setting Writing Standards, 2011–2018, for students in grades 1–12. She has written for a variety of national educational journals and presented often at teaching conferences, but the most fulfilling aspect of her work, by far, was seeing her students succeed.

Andrea lives in Iowa City with Shadow and Sunny, two wild and crazy standard poodles. Her most fulfilling role is that of playing Mary Poppins to beloved grandchildren Katherine and Drew.

More Books from Theme Park Press

Theme Park Press is the largest independent publisher of Disney, Disney-related, and general interest theme park books in the world, with dozens of new releases each year.

Our authors include Disney historians like Jim Korkis and Didier Ghez, Disney animators and artists like Mel Shaw and Eric Larson, and such Disney notables as Van France, Tom Nabbe, and Bill "Sully" Sullivan, as well as many promising first-time authors.

We're always looking for new talent.

In March 2016, we published our 100th title. For a complete catalog, including book descriptions and excerpts, please visit:

ThemeParkPress.com

The Ride Delegate

Disney for the 1%. The rich and famous experience Disney World differently from the rest of us: they're escorted by VIP Tour Guides, elite Cast Members who truly do hold the keys to the kingdom. Annie Salisbury was one of these Cast Members, in charge of making the very best magic for those who could afford it.

themeparkpress.com/books/ride-delegate.htm

Together in the Dream

R.J. painted audio-animatronic figures and "plussed" attractions. Suzanne drove monorails, marched in parades, and entertained as Sleepy the dwarf. Together, the Ogrens brought their unique skills to Walt Disney World's Magic Kingdom during its formative years. This is their story.

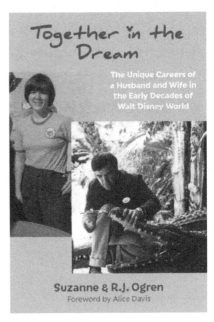

themeparkpress.com/books/together-dream.htm

Sara Earns Her Ears

From Cali to the Castle. For California girl Sara Lopes, it wasn't enough to walk down Walt Disney World's Main Street. She wanted to live there. She got her wish, for a little while, and her secret cast member diary takes you with her from Cali to Cinderella Castle.

themeparkpress.com/books/sara-earns-her.ears.htm

Would You Like Magic with That?

Guests gone wild! What's ground zero at Walt Disney World? Guest Relations. It's where visitors go to cajole, connive, and most of all, complain. Guests cry. They lie. Some even collapse to the floor. For these unhappy campers, Annie Salisbury was the power behind the pixie dust. Her tell-all will shock and amaze.

themeparkpress.com/books/would-you-like-magic-with-that.htm

Two Girls and a Mouse Tale

Elly and Caroline Collins aren't just sisters; they're best friends, too. So when Elly suggested that they join the Disney College Program together, Caroline went right along. They left their family and boyfriends in Colorado for a once-in-a-lifetime opportunity to live, work, and play with Mickey Mouse.

themeparkpress.com/books/two-girls-mouse-tale.htm

From Jungle Cruise Skipper to Disney Legend

Disney Legend William "Sully" Sullivan got his start in 1955 with Walt Disney and Disneyland, taking tickets for the Jungle Cruise. Forty years later he retired as vice-president of Walt Disney World's Magic Kingdom. This is his never-before-told story, in his own words.

themeparkpress.com/books/sully-sullivan-jungle-cruise-legend.htm

Made in the USA
Monee, IL
06 August 2022

11041648R00105